CLARE
RICHMOND

THE
SCAVENGER
MINDSET

RETHINKING
LEADERSHIP TO
UNLOCK THE
UNTAPPED
TALENT WITHIN

The Scavenger Mindset
ISBN 978-1-912300-74-7 (paperback)
eISBN 978-1-912300-75-4

Published in 2022 by Right Book Press
Printed in the UK

A CIP record of this book is available from the British Library.

THE SCAVENGER MINDSET

Contents

Foreword

I've spent my career helping large organisations to do a better job for their customers, or more broadly the people they serve. Organisations that became exceptionally good at it all employ thousands of people, all have highly paid leaders and all have unusual beliefs. These beliefs are what led to their success.

The common belief, even the obvious one, is that to do well you need to do things that benefit you and your organisation. But the organisations I have studied were different. They believed that they're here to do things for others, and so that's what they concentrate on – how do they solve their customers' problems in new and better ways? If they do this well, they believe that the organisation will, in good time, do well too.

In *The Scavenger Mindset*, Clare Richmond has almost magical answers to some important questions. How can communities, apparently with very little, achieve a lot? How can a group with no formal leader, structure or budget make their world better, happier and more productive?

When I first met Clare, she'd come to give me some feedback on an event we'd run. Luckily, I asked

what she was up to. She shared a story about a high
street – her high street – but close to where I lived
too. She talked about the problems it had and the local
shopkeepers wilting under the pressure of better-
resourced national competitors. Then she described
what she'd done about it, feeling her way but confident
in the community's ability to solve the problem. She
wanted to work with the community to find a way to
regain its mojo – to grow its energy and create a sense
of place like it used to have at its best.

The project, as it became, had lifted off with some
evening events, hosted by the independent shops and
cafes that stayed open late and acted as hosts, with
music played by young locals. I knew about it because
my son had played washboard in a three-person skiffle
band and we had gone down to see him, only to get
drawn into the unfolding occasion. As you'll read, that
was part of Clare's plan.

It didn't just work for me; it worked for the high
street and for the community. Over 18 months the
place was transformed, confidence grew, relationships were forged and, as a virtual organisation, the
same kind of success had been achieved that I'd been
advising and writing about. Just as I'd found with large
organisations, making things better outside brings
benefit back inside, to the businesses at the heart of
the high street. It was what I'd witnessed before but
achieved in a very different, even smarter way.

This book is the story of how.

It's full of eyebrow-raising revelations: groups of people solving seriously tough problems, using nothing more than what they had in front of them. Clare shows that having a budget isn't even a nice-to-have – sometimes, it's a best-to-do-without, and why plans and targets can make the plans less likely to be followed and the targets less likely to be achieved.

Becoming a scavenger might sound slightly macabre, but this is about being lean, flexible, creative and resourceful, finding value in what's already there. It is essentially human. It starts not with logic but energy that gets generated by trust – trust that a motivated group of people – and that means any people – can solve tough problems in ways that often have been out of reach or overlooked in more conventional approaches.

It's the sort of behaviour the world needs more of – indeed, it's the sort of book the world needs more of. Well, it did: now it has got one.

So read, enjoy and be inspired to have a go yourself.

Charlie Dawson, founder of The Foundation and co-author (with Seán Meehan) of *The Customer Copernicus: How to Be Customer-led*

Introduction

A scavenger's life

I was the first person in my family *not* to go to university. As I didn't have a career mapped out or a detailed view of where I was heading, I had to engage with the world in a different way to my older siblings. With a few A-levels tucked under my belt, my life was a blank canvas on which I sketched out an impression around 'something to do with communication': it was my dad's suggestion, based on detecting some early signs in me of raw skill in this area. However, having little experience in this field, he could only offer encouragement from the sidelines.

Having a blank canvas in front of you can be incredibly daunting, but can also create a profound sense of freedom. It demands tenacity, flexibility and a resourceful, agile approach – one that hasn't been evident in any formal learning I've experienced. I've had to master the art of working with what's been readily available to me, stretching my imagination about what might be possible, and making the most of resources and opportunities.

When I first moved to London, I didn't know anyone. I had no contacts apart from an elderly aunt who introduced me to a friend who worked in PR. It was a small start, but as it turned out, that was all I needed. I went on to work in marketing media for the next 15 years, building contacts and experience. I began my career in commercial radio, working under the leadership of an extraordinary Canadian, Terry Bates, from whom I learned a lot about energy, determination and professionalism.

At that time, radio was a hotbed of change with new stations being launched, while the industry fought for a bigger slice of the advertising pie. Radio was the underdog to television and print media, but I loved the regional stations that inspired and reflected the communities they served. From these stations I learned about the power of belonging and connection. I became a sales director at a relatively tender age, and recognised the pitfalls of making promises you have little power to keep.

From there I experienced many highs and lows, working across the launch of cable TV, including the infamous Live TV under the joint leadership of former *Sun* editor Kelvin MacKenzie and broadcaster Janet Street-Porter.

When I look back over those 15 years, it feels like I lived in a pinball machine, ricocheting from one role to another in a wide range of media, from publishing to posters and many more in between. As a result, I've never been under any illusion about how quickly life can change, so I learned to keep my antennae firmly tuned to the here and now. It's not a perspective that's easily accommodated in a hierarchical world but one which, I've come to realise, helps people to lead in turbulent times. The high level of uncertainty I experienced was in complete contrast to the certainty and control that the leaders of the companies I worked with were expected to exercise. It was all about targets and being seen to achieve them at any cost. In my experience, this frequently led to overstressed, anxious teams who skated on thin ice to keep their jobs, while the reality of the challenges they faced and the emergence of new opportunities were overlooked or dismissed.

Throughout my life I've had a deep-rooted feeling that I'll be OK. I haven't always been justified in feeling this, but it has helped me nonetheless to maintain a sense of balance at difficult times, and stay relatively sane amid the rollercoaster of rapid change. Whatever life throws at me, I've believed I'll have the resources to cope. This level of 'OK-ness' has nurtured my positive, forward-thinking mindset – one that has proved to be vital to me as a parent, going through divorce and building my own business.

I believe it was this mindset that led me to an experience that changed my life and outlook on leadership – one that came about in an informal, almost accidental way. Having lived in America for a couple of years I returned home, a new mum, to contemplate a new phase of life, with fresh, star-spangled eyes on the world. One of the first things to strike me was how down-at-heel our local high-street community was looking: used to American-style customer service, the shops seemed lacklustre to me by comparison, and many seemed to be struggling.

Without much thought about what might be involved, I began to consider what could help or might be possible. I started with nothing: no resources, funding, permission, experience or much idea about how to do it.

Strangely, that turned out to be an advantage.

After 18 months, the results had far exceeded my expectations, and taught me so much about leading from a ground-up perspective. After that initial success, several local authorities and town centres approached me to help replicate the experience in their own high streets. That was when I experienced the challenges of implementing a grassroots approach in a top-down environment. There was certainly the will and potential in each and every community I worked with, but the top-down approach stifled that, with the local authority clinging onto the project's reins and failing to engage with the considerable resources that existed. I felt that this approach skimmed the surface, and focused primarily on meeting predetermined outcomes. I found it increasingly frustrating that opportunities were often missed, and underlying challenges went unaddressed. When you're aiming to deliver a change in behaviour and kick-start regeneration, big budgets lead to overinflated ambition, which in turn puts pressure on everyone involved to achieve something that may not last or be relevant.

After a few years of involvement with a series of these projects, I embarked on an MA in Creative Leadership to explore how I might translate my experiences and insights to help leaders adopt a more productive, less top-down approach. This gave my experience a framework that broadened its context, and fuelled my sense of possibility.

For example, little did I know, when I embarked on my high-street regeneration project (see Chapter 1), that I was actually tackling what's known as a 'wicked problem': one that:

- is characterised by complexity
- has no simple answer
- involves a myriad of agendas and stakeholders
- has no clear end point.

As I discovered, a wicked problem requires a completely different leadership approach, demanding a mindset that I found to be more instinctive. It requires active engagement, broader perspectives and a clear vision that's brought to life not by detailed documents and strategic plans, but by action and an environment that enables learning and creativity.

Here, not knowing is to be expected – and can even be an asset. I discovered a feeling of belonging in the world of wicked problems.

Of course, there are problems that require a more conventional approach, known as 'tame problems': these are likely to be extremely complicated but solvable by using an existing template. They need expertise, experience and a leadership style where a 'spreadsheet mentality' is both appropriate and effective. However, whether we like it or not, we're living in an increasingly wicked world – and we need to adopt a different mindset to deal with it.

I created the 'scavenger mindset' as a way to both encourage leaders to be more 'wicked', and help to successfully navigate uncertainty.

This book sets out to introduce the scavenger mindset: what it is, why adopting it will help you gain a competitive and personal advantage, and how it can inspire you to look again and look deeper at what you already have.

Small in size and hopefully significant in nature, this book has been designed to encourage readers to reimagine what might be possible despite the turbulent, complex times in which we're living. The scavenger mindset is a ground-up perspective on leadership that seeks to strengthen leaders from the inside-out. It's all about showing that it doesn't take a lot to make a massive difference; just that there is something different that can be done.

Most importantly, it will show you that you already have exactly what you need in a wicked world – and by focusing on that and learning how to release it, you'll be able to achieve far more with very much less.

It's time to release your inner scavenger!

How to spot a wicked problem

Wicked problems were first cited by Rittel and Webber (1973) to distinguish between the different approaches needed to solve different types of problems.

In addition to tame and wicked problems, there's a third type: a critical problem, which requires a more commanding leadership style. For many academics, wicked problems require leadership, while tame problems are more about management and process. The approach required for wicked problems is counter-intuitive to what's conventionally expected of leaders, which is to wield authority through being decisive. The pressure to act decisively often means leaders try to solve problems as if they were tame, but they end up failing to address the reality of the situation.

Keith Grint, Emeritus Professor (formerly Professor of Public Leadership and Management) at Warwick Business School, reinforces the importance of collective thinking when it comes to wicked problems, and 'a transfer of authority from the individual to the collective, because only a collective can hope to address the problem' (Grint and Holt 2012). Wicked problems require a mindset shift and an ability to suspend judgement in favour of real-time learning – focusing on the here and now – harnessing the widest possible perspectives, and dealing with emerging problems and opportunities as they arise.

Wicked problems can be found pretty much everywhere: they pop up like a game of Whack-a-Mole. If we're not careful, we can expend a lot of energy firefighting and trying to contain problems. We need to stretch our thinking and get comfortable with conflict, chaos, change and challenge. I believe that by embracing uncertainty we can lessen our anxiety, release our creative spirit and gain a huge competitive advantage. Consider what type of problem you're facing, and be alert to wicked ones sneaking into even the most tame-looking situation.

Here's how to spot a wicked problem:

- There are no clear answers.
- There are multiple stakeholders and agendas.
- You only begin to understand the problem once you act.
- It's dynamic and changeable.
- You need to work with what's in the here and now, not with what has been done before.
- There's no end point at which the problem is solved.

Watching the huge response to a simple, home-made initiative to reinstate the value of the high street back in 2009 shifted something significant in my mind. It wasn't just that we'd brought people together to create change for themselves; neither was it that we'd had such an impact when we'd started with so little.

It was the revelation that much more could be accomplished when you focus on the beginning, not just the end, and that the only thing that matters is that people feel capable of facing whatever happens or emerges.

I didn't set out to do anything other than have a go at something that felt really important to me. This book doesn't seek to offer neat answers to the challenges and complexities we currently face – that would be pointless, as there aren't any. But it does provide a preview of the incredible things which can be accomplished when you invest in the people and resources that are right in front of you.

I've also included four 'scavenger pioneer' stories throughout the book: stories about leaders I've been lucky enough to meet over the years who have taken a similar approach to me, but have gone on to achieve far more with it. Even though they've tackled very different challenges, they share humble beginnings and common leadership traits. They have all displayed courage, imagination and perseverance and found ways to motivate others, bringing people with them to participate and contribute at remarkable levels to help achieve something incredible.

These scavenger pioneers are just the tip of the iceberg, but their stories give us all hope. They illustrate why we already have what we need to deal with uncertainty and to meet and even exceed our goals.

1 A scavenger on the high street

Even before the financial meltdown of 2008, a stroll past your local shops would have provided plenty of evidence that the high street was in crisis. The purveyors of 'local and convenience' shopping no longer occupied the high street and had been slowly replaced by online shopping and out-of-town shopping centres, with their price promises, huge product range and free parking.

The effect on the high street at the centre of my community in north London, which consisted mostly of small, independent shops, was becoming increasingly obvious. On the surface, there didn't appear to be a comprehensive fightback in the face of such sophisticated competition, but deep down, the story was even more worrying.

I had no experience of running a small business, but the demise of my local high street felt like an important enough issue for me to explore potential solutions. It seemed to me that there was still an important, even vital, role for the high street to play; it just needed to be rediscovered and possibly reshaped.

With no money or resources of any kind, I needed to work with what was available.

The obvious place to start was with the business community.

My experience steered me towards the belief that the challenge was a marketing one, but I was in no position to impose this view or catalyse action because of it. I needed to introduce myself to these businesses, and get to know what was really going on for them.

To help with the introductions, I began by working with a local retailer, the owner of an independent Budgens franchise. We sent out an invitation to the businesses for an event to discuss how to improve the fortunes of the high street: an opportunity to start conversations with as many businesses as possible and gauge the level of interest. Three people turned up to the first meeting, and one of them was me.

It wasn't a promising start, but gradually the numbers grew. Through this process something deeper emerged, revealing a challenge I hadn't anticipated. I was met with resignation, shrugs of despondency and a pervasive sense of fatigue. Even the most enterprising businesses were aware that alone, they simply didn't have the influence necessary to change customer behaviour to the extent required. The whole concept of the high street in the UK seemed to be frozen in a bygone age, underpinned by a malaise within the business community.

It felt important to bring businesses together, to reignite a sense of possibility and power. The invitation to these businesses hadn't been one to sit passively and listen, but to be a part of a group that could take ownership, learn about the context, exchange ideas and act. There were no neat answers, but some important questions to be asked.

I was surprised by how disparate the business community seemed to be. Again, I had made some lazy assumptions. I had assumed there would be a sense of camaraderie through shared experience, familiarity, even friendships. Instead, I discovered that few of the business owners knew each other and that initially, many were suspicious of one another – particularly those operating in the same sector. In fact, they were only united by their condemnation of the local authority: the claimed source of their woes.

While rents, rates and parking were legitimate causes for concern, I was keen to avoid fixating on these. We had no real power in this area, and I could see how disappearing down this rabbit hole could undermine our efforts and bring the whole thing to a shuddering standstill. It was important to park these issues and focus on what could be possible.

To have any chance of building something positive and vibrant, we needed to address the feeling of powerlessness and disconnection. I hoped to show the businesses that despite these limitations, something could be done: that together, they had the power and resources to act independently – without the need for local authority intervention.

In fact, my view was that action would be possible only if we didn't have initial involvement from the local authority. There were never any promises made or ambitious targets set; they wouldn't have been relevant at this stage when we needed action to encourage new behaviours and learn. It became a focused process of discovery and collective learning around the question of how to make the high street valuable again.

Starting small, starting somewhere

Within a couple of months, 25 businesses had committed to doing something together, paying whatever they could afford on a monthly basis. Working with a local graphic designer, we created a collective brand logo and templates for colourful and bold promotional material that reflected the community, and would be inexpensive to update.

With a high street that had lost its value to the local community, the starting point was to invite them back to the high street, much like a host inviting guests for dinner. Our focus wouldn't be on selling but engagement: inviting them to a late-night event offering free entertainment accessible to all, and allowing the business community to welcome their customers to browse, chat and enjoy refreshments in their stores. The aim was to give people a good reason to return – not by telling them to 'save our shops' or 'love your locals', but by building relationships that would stand the test of time. The theory was: do something nice for someone, and they're more likely to go out of their way for you.

This strategy had emerged when it became clear that the businesses were no longer in a position to meet conventional customer needs, but were in a great position to meet community needs – which have the benefit of being timeless. No one wants to live in a ghost town; people want to feel as if they belong, and this is best provided at a point of contact in the community, by the community.

I argued that anything the businesses could do to promote this feeling of belonging would be of innate value, and wouldn't require hefty budgets. The value was in the connections and relationships the businesses could nurture within the community.

A little liberation goes a long way

When you have little to work with, you need to be resourceful, enterprising and pragmatic. There are things you simply can't do, but there is still a lot that can be accomplished.

We had the freedom to try things out, test and learn what worked and what didn't. As a result, I developed a strong can-do/will-do attitude. As soon as the first actions were agreed, I began to consider how we could enrol support beyond the business community. To maximise that impact, we needed the wider community to become involved and connect them to their high street.

Wherever it's located, every community will have catalyst hubs: groups or individuals who have something to offer and share. My children were small at the time, so I had access to a network of parent and carer friends with an enormous range of experience and high-level skills (any playground will offer up the same potential). I also had a great babysitting network of young people with plenty of energy and ideas.

Early on, I'd involved a friend of mine with amazing retail and design experience, and together we recruited a group of babysitters with whom we worked closely to become our 'brand ambassadors' and promotion team.

(In my case I was fortunate to have access to a wide range of talent and skills from the playground parents and carers, but in every community I have ever worked, I have met individuals and groups who are resourceful and capable of amazing innovation and support. I am confident where ever you are, whatever the circumstances, there is hidden talent to tap into.)

It was time well invested; their energy and enthusiasm became a key part of our success. With the same aim, I contacted local schools and spoke to music teachers about organising children's involvement: in our first event, they sang carols in the centre of the high street. Apart from being festive, my hope was that involving children would naturally bring out parents and siblings who would help to spread the word.

To launch the event, we used a simple teaser campaign and placed A4 laminated posters in shop windows showing the date of the event and asking: 'Have you got your bag yet?' We had T-shirts made for shop owners with the same question printed on them – a really simple device, but it worked. The campaign punched well above its weight, creating curiosity and sparking conversations inside shops about what the bag was and what it was for, it being the first merchandise we produced. Not only did it help to bring in some income while promoting the project and participating businesses, but it also helped a campaign to reduce the use of plastic bags. In a similar vein, we organised a treasure hunt, placing objects in the window of every participating shop to encourage people to walk round the high street and visit each one.

None of these ideas were groundbreaking, but they didn't need to be – they just needed to work.

If a job's worth doing, it's worth doing (even badly)

Despite the increasing buzz that was coming from the businesses, I was extremely nervous on the night of our first event. Of course there were naysayers, the 'it won't work, we've tried that before' gang. Then there were my own feelings of recklessness:

was I leading everyone up the garden path?

The key consolation was that I had always been explicit about the aim: to take action to learn, slowly but surely. No one was under any illusion or expecting miracles; we were just hoping that people would be curious and invested enough to come along. Whatever the outcome, we'd learn something valuable.

It was a cold, dark, drizzly December night: people could have been easily forgiven for staying at home (and by 6.30 pm, I was beginning to wish I had). I remember standing outside one of the shops on the main drag of the high street, feeling slightly queasy. I could see our young brand ambassadors dressed up as angels, doing a great job of chatting to people as they got off buses on their way home from work, but could discern little else of note. But almost imperceptibly, a crowd began to form in front of the town hall, ready for carol singing at 7 pm.

Later, while walking through the streets, I saw huddles of people taking part in our treasure hunt, peering in shop windows and searching for the object that didn't belong; then, more often than not, wandering inside to take a look and meet the owner. By 10 pm many of these windows had steamed up, the shops were still filled with people, the sound of music and laughter permeating the cold night air long after the event had officially ended.

The evening seemed to have been a success and, even though it was a small triumph, it had a surpris-

A SCAVENGER ON THE HIGH STREET

ingly profound effect on me. It proved to me that following my instinct, having a go and working hard to achieve something that mattered, worked. It didn't matter that I wasn't a fully formed community engagement person, a shop owner or even anything to do with retail – I distinctly remember the glow of growing possibility.

However, the real test was yet to come. How would the businesses react? What had their experience been? When we met again the following month, the shops were still buzzing, with some reporting record sales on the night. Just as important were the conversations they had had with customers and others who had never been in their shops before. It demonstrated to the businesses that they had influence: they had come together, taken action and the community had responded. The high street had been a place most would walk through to get home and visit to shop occasionally. Now new connections had been made – a feeling of belonging ignited.

It was a promising start.

A chord of connectivity

Fast-forward 18 months: we had hosted more than 21 community events and attracted many new businesses and organisations, including film nights at the local library. We went on to host a summer music festival with local musicians and bands; curated a month of green activities; a sensational fashion week that culminated in a fundraising event for breast cancer, with a catwalk featuring local fashion and health and beauty practitioners treating the locals to an evening of love and attention.

The brand we had created was being increasingly recognised and warmly received. When we felt we'd earned the right to go online, we applied for funding from the local authority to create a website: its launch was a revelation. It showed we'd hit a chord of connectivity within the community, as the platform was used increasingly for more than simply looking up the high-street businesses – we received enquiries about all manner of local issues and interests.

I learned so much from this about the hidden potential within a community: by taking small steps, how you build capacity and confidence that creates the foundation for something meaningful to grow. Most of all, I saw that when people feel valued and connected, it fuels ingenuity, engagement and energy.

By the end of the project we had worked with nearly 200 businesses and organisations, created a platform that the community wanted to engage with on their own terms and sparked a feeling of optimism that lasted long after we stepped away. With an initial budget of £15,000, we had made an impact on the community and demonstrated how successful a small, grassroots initiative can be when tackling complex challenges and overcoming deep-rooted problems.

To this day people still remember the events, our bags are still seen in the area and the community continues to have great affection for the initiative, which sparked other community-inspired events. On reflection, one of the reasons for the initiative's success was that there was very little to lose, but a lot to gain – a simple equation that invites high levels of innovation and learning. There was just enough structure to build momentum, and a clear sense of direction that became the reference point for everything we did.

Despite the informality, we couldn't afford to waste time or money, which brought a particular energy and focus to the group. While no one was demanding that targets be met, motivation was self-generated and fuelled by confidence that grew in tandem with our success and learning.

That experience has stayed with me – and inspired me to promote the benefits of this ground-up approach to leadership when navigating complex problems.

Ground-up versus top-down leadership

The lessons I learned were amplified and reinforced in the work I went on to do in other boroughs, town centres and high streets.

My next project involved a neighbouring local authority which had heard about the success of the high-street initiative. I was asked to deliver a talk to its business community, in the hope of igniting interest in replicating our approach. I was delighted to be asked, felt positive about what could be accomplished, and keen to share the insights we had about how businesses could benefit.

Before my talk, the leader of the council warned me that it had no money to contribute to an initiative. He was surprised to discover that I was pleased – even relieved – to hear that. As mentioned previously, for this approach to work, it needs to be driven and owned by businesses and/or the community – not the local authority.

My talk went well and just as I was receiving applause, the council leader came to the front of the room to join me. Before I could do anything to stop him, he pledged a significant fund to kick-start a project in their high street. In that one well-meaning but perhaps, in my view, miscalculated announce-ment, the opportunity to replicate my approach was stymied. The focus turned to how the money should be spent, and what followed was months of wrangling and discussions about hanging baskets, benches and painting shop fronts – all of which had value, but lost the opportunity to galvanise the community to drive and own an initiative.

At around the same time, I was commissioned by another London authority to write a report on their five town centres, identifying where I saw the challenges and opportunities in setting up a similar initiative. These locations were culturally very different but all had people, organisations and businesses capable of leading change and creating something significant. Critical to that were the expectations of the authority's roles and responsibilities, and the chance to develop on-the-ground ownership.

One of the town centres had once been at the epicentre of the London riots in the 2010s. My work started a year later, but the scars and bruises remained. To offset this and inject some positive energy, the local authority commissioned a piece of wall art, created with the help of local children. It asked the question: 'What's happening here?' The idea was that every week events would be added to create a buzz and promote local activity.

On paper this looked like a good idea – but to the people I met, this mural became a massive thorn in their side, a constant reminder not of the vibrancy of their community, but of the disconnect between local authority and community. Those I spoke to were insulted that the local authority hadn't seen the potential within their own community to create something meaningful for it. For the people I spoke to, this seemed misguided on so many levels. The question was left hanging above the high street, forgotten or ignored.

However, just round the corner in a small side street, people had painted a wall emblazoned with raw and moving words: a testament to their resilience, determination and love for their community. The local authority ignored it and eventually it was whitewashed.

This sickened me. Whether it was their intention or not – and I can't imagine it was – in this one apparently thoughtless act of social vandalism, they managed to both dismiss and undermine the voices of the community and cause an even wider chasm to open up between council and community. It was a prime example of not seeing or valuing the potential that exists, not investing the necessary time, or perhaps just being too fearful to engage with it. In not doing so, the cost was great and set back community relations even further.

Over the next few years I worked across a wide range of high-street regeneration and community-building projects, from one-off advisory roles to consultancy, including being chosen as a specialist advisor to 'Design for London', the Mayor of London's high-street regeneration project, inspired by the initiative led by expert retail consultant and creative agency founder, Mary Portas. I also appeared on an economic panel for the London Assembly, and was invited to do a talk on high-street regeneration on Radio 4's *Four Thought*. My work took me into a wide range of communities, meeting businesses and working alongside teams of consultants and experts brought together to help town centres find a new, positive future and kick-start local economies.

On paper, this made sense. It was a response that ticked a lot of boxes, but as I was to discover, this top-down approach failed to build the capacity necessary for long-term, viable regeneration. Each project began with a sizeable budget, and an assumption that the solution would be both to use the expertise around the conference table, and that the project's aims would be met within a specified timeframe.

Once there was agreement on the plan, it was launched into the community – but there was little in the way of meaningful community engagement.

As with any family, business or organisation, every community has its own DNA made up of its heritage, geography, culture, businesses and narrative – and these need to be honoured. Whatever the scheme or initiative, taking time to establish good working relationships is fundamental to long-term success, to build foundations that hold when things go wrong, and maintain momentum when the initial project is finished. Every community has individuals, groups or organisations able to lead or contribute to a grassroots initiative, but time needs to be invested to establish relationships that can work.

This is where the magic lies – but it's an area I felt was missed too frequently or glossed over.

Engagement is a two-way street

One of the London town centres I worked with as part of the Design for London initiative in 2010 had a well-known drama school in its area. I understood the power of involving local people and groups – particularly young people – in bringing life to a community project, so I approached them and met with owners and students to discuss possible collaborations. We discussed ways in which they could inject energy and create interest with flash mobs, dancing, live art in shop windows, themes, readings, storytelling and plays. The signs were encouraging, but often in my experience, the bureaucratic process unwittingly stifles much of the grassroots potential.

Despite a promising start, there appeared to be no evidence that the potential in this relationship was fulfilled once our involvement in the project was over – and to this day, I still feel that those students were let down. Perhaps it didn't fit with the project's expectations, but this was never explained to me. Once our time on the project was over, it was over. For me this remains a sad example of a 'spreadsheet mentality' getting in the way of an opportunity to leave an inspiring legacy, and to connect the high street with the community in the long term.

An ongoing challenge which raised its head a number of times was how to address issues raised by the public, particularly if they were critical. Building positive relationships is key to long-term success and sustainability, so avoidance of any criticism or negative feedback is unhelpful in the extreme. In any situation where you require something from someone, however large or small, consideration needs to be given to how to communicate this to ensure the best possible response and outcome.

There were many similar examples during the course of my work, where discussions in the vacuum of the office failed to consider how communication and engagement would land in the wider community. This is a quick way to create a disconnect: if people don't feel involved or connected, they either won't bother or will just do the bare minimum, or if they have the energy, find reasons to complain.

Engagement is a two-way street, and only effective if all parties are considered. I've attended many meetings with local authorities and the local business community, where even the set-up of the room sets the tone for the meeting. Local authority representatives sat behind desks as on a panel, splitting the space in two and implying parent–child roles. On one side, the public, expecting the local authority to meet their needs; and on the other, the local authority feeling obliged to do so, and either becoming defensive or servile.

Very few of these exchanges felt productive or led to satisfying outcomes, and many resulted in either the proverbial 'can being kicked down the road', or promises made that were unlikely to be fulfilled. These exchanges aren't confined to local government, but are clearly marked there. The scene is set where one 'side' is left feeling let down, and the other overburdened with the weight of the unachiev–able. Parity needs to be restored for a narrative to emerge that is more involving, encourages greater spread of responsibility and so opportunity, where collective learning emerges around a set direction.

Over my years of working in the field of town-centre regeneration, the question that kept arising for me was: 'What is the long-term legacy of this project?'

Most of the 12 town centres that were awarded funding during the Mary Portas initiative met with similar problems and disappointing outcomes. The £100,000 fund was a huge amount not to show results, and needed to please a myriad of different people with varying agendas.

Plus councils still bore the brunt of responsibil-ity. One Margate resident felt that the money hadn't made much difference to his town centre. That had already been achieved with a far bigger budget, when the area was upgraded in response to the building of the Turner Contemporary art gallery. He told the *Daily Mail* that the success of Margate's regeneration was due in the main to:

… lots of gentle interventions of people starting a street market, starting their own events. Those are really important because those are the things that really bring the place to life and are still going. (Robinson 2021)

That's what matters most in the long term.

What happens when the circus leaves town?

The conventional approach to regenerative initiatives has a beginning and end. A vision is outlined, strategy developed and end-of-project summary produced to establish that the predetermined targets were indeed satisfactorily met. When the boxes have been ticked and final presentation of results delivered, distributed and filed, the initiative is considered done and dusted.

In each project I worked on, there were clear deadlines and ambitious targets, including reducing unemployment and vacancy rates, and increasing footfall. They're all worthy and highly valuable targets, but how realistic were they in a timeframe of less than two years? What was left behind: a newly invigorated high street, with renewed value to the community? Often it was just a few soggy flyers adorned with council logos, a smattering of press photos of an Easter Bunny parade, some newly laid pavements, flowers and repainted shop fronts, which no doubt improved the appearance of the high street, but not much else.

The expectation remained that local authorities were in charge of regenerating high streets, that the solutions were 'out there', and a sense that the authorities had done what was required of them: file closed. And next year, or the year after that? What if there was still a problem? Would the authority be recalled to reopen the regeneration file and start again?

That's not how wicked problems work, and high-street regeneration is nothing if not wicked. It's a 24/7 rolling beast that needs a constant level of response and learning. There are no easy answers. That's why grand promises and ambitious visions so often fall down. The weight of delivery is often in the hands of the wrong people doing the right job. The conventional tame approach promises much, yet delivers little – and those that came to fix the problem leave to a chorus of shame.

Wicked problems need a different mindset: one where the focus is not on producing a set of results, but on creative, critical thinking. Any 'expert' involvement is more of a catalyst and occasional support rather than a driver. Councillor Reece Pugh described the Margate scheme as giving confidence to the town (Robinson 2021), and confidence is the key to creating long-term change. It's so important to spark a conversation, build community around the challenge.

The starting point should be to ask a question to excite wider involvement, challenge new ideas and perspectives, and build confidence and capacity from within.

I'd like to say that the high street I worked with back in 2008 is now thriving, but the lockdowns of the past two years have taken a toll. However, I was pleased to learn through a conversation at the beginning of 2022 with my old colleague, Helene Connolly (who still lives in the area), that in common with many other communities, their community spirit was reawakened during the pandemic.

She said: 'It felt as if the community quickly remembered how to behave like a community.' Connectivity was re-established, and businesses were quick to act in enterprising and resourceful ways. For a long period after the main project activity ceased, that renewed sense of community had been enough to restore footfall, spark new initiatives and attract new businesses to the area, most of which are still in operation. Most importantly, people didn't feel let down or fobbed off.

Something exciting had happened, and for many the domino effect was tangible.

The high street is, of course, a microcosm of our society: it mirrors many of the challenges and opportunities found in any organisation. Its governance is hierarchical, with different departmental functions dealing with different community aspects, often in silos. Communities are places that need things 'doing to them', requiring high-level intervention, controls and stipulations – echoes found in many leadership approaches taken by leaders with their teams.

Scavenger beginnings

What I find the most striking about the conventional, top-down approach is the waste. In the projects I worked on, there were countless meetings to ensure we were on track, and conversations to ensure the right guidelines were being followed or the right logo used. These overshadowed the time spent on building community relationships and facilitating the best way forward.

This was when the scavenger mindset emerged. I experienced such a contrast in approaches between my own and top-down:

- Mine starts with a question, finds a goal without any set way of meeting it and works with what's readily available.
- Top-down begins with an ambitious goal that creates big promises and features detailed plans of how it will all be achieved, but fails to engage ground-up ownership to build community and carry it forward.

Ultimately, I felt the obsession with being certain and in control was damaging our ability to think imaginatively and engage with reality. And the way in which our roles and responsibilities were set up was actually preventing us from working productively.

I concluded that we needed to rethink what a useful leadership role can be in fast-changing times, where command-and-control no longer works. An approach that is less wasteful encourages leaders to:

- look again and deeper at what they already have
- be upfront and explicit around uncertainty
- build community to cope with multilayered challenges.

During my MA, so much of what I'd experienced in regeneration and change projects began to fall into place. A thought-provoking combination of complexity theory, mediation and creativity helped to bring all the elements of my experience together to become the scavenger mindset. I recognised that the more complex life becomes, the more entrenched we become. The more we're unwilling to step outside our comfort zones, the more we need to do so.

This makes complete sense, as we're not wired to enjoy feeling uncomfortable; we're encouraged to stick with what we know, and be sure about what we say. Happily, there are some small and easy ways to begin to adopt a mindset that can help us navigate these wicked times – and even learn to enjoy it.

After all, so much ahead of us is uncertain, and we need to be better equipped to deal with that. Adopting a scavenger mindset helps us to keep our balance when everything around us is wobbling.

2 What is the scavenger mindset?

The *Collins English Dictionary* defines 'scavenger' as 'a person who searches for and collects discarded items'.

In the animal kingdom, the scavenger doesn't have a particularly good reputation: it conjures up images of hyenas and vultures. But for humans, it's much broader than that. I define it as:

Scavenger: someone who is able to see the value in all people and resources, working imaginatively and intelligently with what's already available.

Scavengers are likely to be highly efficient, resourceful and innovative. My definition extends to *how* the scavenger operates:

- scoping out opportunities and challenges
- focusing on what's in front of them
- making the most of what's available in the context of the goal they want to reach.

The scavenger mindset is about letting go of unnecessary meetings, weighty documents and meaningless targets; focusing instead on where the greatest influence and impact lies.

It:

+ cares little for what has gone before
+ shrugs in the face of conventional wisdom
+ is hardwired to work in the here and now
+ looks beyond boundaries
+ knocks down walls to unearth hidden potential
+ has a forensic focus on learning.

The scavenger mindset sits comfortably with not knowing, and managing the unexpected. Fuelled by imagination and valuing what others may overlook, it builds community around uncertainty and innovation. It's a warrior mindset that punches well above its weight, needing far less to achieve much more.

In its simplest form, the scavenger mindset is about the ability to create and nurture an environment in which anyone and everyone can contribute their best. It believes that what we have is all we need. In the face of adversity, those with the scavenger mindset ask: 'So what? What action do we need to take, what do we need to find out?'

It:

- makes new connections
- prompts new ideas
- is driven by good questions, clear direction and a determination to learn
- sees the potential in everyone
- finds the ideal conditions in which to release and nurture this potential.

At its core, the scavenger mindset:

- is driven by questions
- inspires new thinking
- creates connections
- focuses on providing ideal conditions to nurture and release talent.

This doesn't mean mistakes don't happen. It just means that challenges aren't avoided or ignored. Valuing people's commitment and involvement, the scavenger mindset creates a sense of belonging and ownership that distributes responsibility and awakens collective opportunity.

Essential beliefs of the scavenger leader

- Everyone has potential, given the right conditions and tools.
- Leaders don't have all the answers, and shouldn't be gatekeepers.
- Small actions lead to bigger impact and meaningful change.
- The more the merrier – except in governance, where less is more.
- Creative critical thinking is essential to innovation, and requires a safe space to flourish.

Scavenger leaders have a 'can-do, will-do' attitude

The scavenger mindset can be found in all walks of life. It's evident everywhere, from the playground to the boardroom. From 'jumpers for goalposts' to managing a crisis, the scavenger mindset can leapfrog assumptions to find resourceful ways in which to solve a problem or meet new challenges.

Limitations are often the key to innovation. Children are natural scavengers: they make the most of their surroundings, and find ways to entertain themselves. They solve problems through wit and intelligence, often to get what they want from their parents and carers. They're curious, persistent and naturally creative. These are important qualities to hold on to when dealing with wicked problems.

In their book *Frugal Innovation: How to Do More with Less*, Navi Radjou and Jaideep Prabhu (2016) explore how these qualities exist throughout the developing world. With very limited resources, people find extraordinarily innovative solutions to the tough challenges they face. From a tailor creating a refrigerator that doesn't require electricity, to using bumps in the road to create energy, you can see that the scavenger mindset is alive and well, and being powerfully applied.

It also can be seen at work at the epicentre of a crisis or natural disaster. Survivors quickly self-organise, pool resources, assess where the need is greatest and support may lie. With extraordinary ingenuity, people demonstrate real leadership skills and incredible enterprise. The scavenger response is consistently more powerful and effective than the top-down approach, which is often weighed down and burdened by bureaucracy.

In her book *Leadership and the New Science* (2006), Margaret Wheatley recounts how, in the aftermath of the 2005 Hurricane Katrina disaster in New Orleans, USA, it was the grassroots communities that were saving lives and supporting each other, while emergency responders were stuck in a hotel room, going through health and safety issues. Given the right conditions, people are naturally capable, resourceful and innovative. Throughout every community and organisation, people show their scavenger spirit.

Often operating under the radar, these people have influence, know how to build community, and are able to galvanise and support others.

I've been constantly reminded of the inexhaustible levels of ingenuity, resourcefulness and organisational skills shown by people when the right conditions are in place. There are everyday examples everywhere that show that, uninstructed, someone has taken the initiative to set up a scheme, project or group, bringing people together to address a particular challenge or need.

In my own neighbourhood I can think of half a dozen examples of people who've had a positive impact: setting up gardening groups, choirs, support groups, boxing clubs, mentoring, childcare, art and craft groups and amateur dramatic clubs. Their ability to put their ideas into action and motivate people to join them, without any of the usual enticements, is impressive. Managing volunteers requires a particular skill, and the ties that bind have to be deep to be effective. The Covid-19 pandemic has revealed this hidden ability in people, time and again. People respond, commit time and effort, display an enormous range of skills to achieve a goal – and most importantly, seem to gain something significant in the process.

In every community I've worked with, many examples of this have emerged:

- the mother who ran a gardening group

- the gruff cafe owner who discreetly offered a safe haven, even breakfast, to many local youths
- a garage owner who welcomed local car enthusiasts to drop by for coffee once a week, and provided an important sanctuary for an elderly man with dementia
- the network of parents and carers looking after each other's children, as well as caring for the elderly and vulnerable.

In their book, *The Abundant Community: Awakening the Power of Families and Neighborhoods* (2010), John McKnight and Peter Block argue that for years, primary care was the function and instinct of communities, but that has been lost through being outsourced to organisations with a less hands-on and flexible approach. These small, informal examples of connectivity, ingenuity and leadership have a powerful impact.

The scavenger mindset values the person, not the title

Over the years, I've met so many impressive people who've had a similar positive influence on the people they work with and for: a quality that's often undervalued in the boardroom. For example, the front-line workers in local authorities or housing associations tasked with maintaining good community relations, often in the face of hostility and disappointment.

One such front-line worker I met achieved good community relations in difficult times of change by simply being open, communicative, kind and resourceful. Her approach was to treat bad news in the same way as good news, keeping people informed and being accessible for any questions or concerns. Often the biggest challenges she faced were not of her or her team's making, but as a result of changes passed down from head office, from those seemingly unaware of the impact their instructions would have, and simply not understanding enough about her experience. Her insights and ideas weren't sought, so were lost to the organisation, creating a disconnect that undermined how valued she felt, and losing the organisation vital on-the-ground information.

Another example is of a young man who ran a highly creative youth community space: he saw beyond the sometimes aggressive, defensive facades of the young people he met, to the hopeful children they once were: the would-be scientist, footballer, teacher, explorer, doctor or inventor who, in primary school, had had a clear sense of who they could be and the adventure life might hold but, by the age of 14, had lost this sense of possibility. He worked to provide an environment that could help them find their way back to those early signs of optimism and, most importantly, keep the faith that they could. He demonstrated that it didn't take a lot to make a massive difference to someone, but it's all too easy to let people fall through the cracks and lose their potential forever.

The Modello Housing and Homestead Project

One of the most astonishing examples of the scavenger mindset and community-building is the Modello Housing and Homestead Project, south of Miami in the USA. It was undertaken by psychologist Dr Roger Mills, who had worked in some of America's most deprived housing estates in the 1980s (Pranksy 2011).

Mills had been appointed after previous government-sponsored schemes had failed to make the hoped-for impact. His approach seemed eccentric to many: he insisted on spending time in the community, just getting to know the area and becoming familiar with the residents before taking any action or making any decisions.

His approach was predicated on the belief that the answers to the community's problems lay within it – and that with the right support, the members of the community were best placed to change their lives and circumstances. He knew that until people could think differently about themselves, no amount of external intervention would make the necessary difference.

Modello was a scary place, almost lawless. Mills was an unassuming, white, middle-class man who initially stuck out there, but despite strange looks and sometimes hostility, he became a regular visitor and an unthreatening presence. After a while he started to make progress and meaningful connections with a few key people within the community. They agreed to work alongside him, and together they went on to transform the community and the lives and expectations of the people within it.

The women Mills initially worked with went on to help the neighbouring communities find their potential, and bring back hope. It took a belief in people and time to build relationships that could drive change from within, but the project is a great example of why this is all so valuable.

CoderDojo

A similar approach was taken by James Whelton, founder of a highly successful coding club, CoderDojo.

Whelton believed that asking for government funding would risk slowing down progress, introducing too much bureaucracy and expending energy in the wrong places. The CoderDojo movement started as open-source and grew quickly. It became a national and international phenomenon, attracting thousands of young people to learn coding – and for many, to find an activity they could excel at outside of the educational curriculum.

Central to the success of CoderDojo was building a sense of community from within. They relied on volunteers to run the clubs, and over time the children who attended became the volunteers, being trained on site and proud to be champions of the ecosystem that had been so brilliantly constructed.

Launched in July 2011, there are now more than 1,900 verified CoderDojo clubs in 93 countries. For many scavenger leaders like Whelton, sustainability is achieved through creating a sense of ownership and value, and progress made by keeping on the outskirts of the establishment, where there is scope to think differently and move quickly.

The simple reality is that with wicked problems in uncertain times, no one person will have the answer – and there may not even be any simple answers. In such cases, expertise is often irrelevant and can be misguided.

The Good Judgment Project

University of Pennsylvania professors Philip Tetlock, Barbara Mellers and Don Moore's Good Judgment Project was designed to understand the impact of the 'expert' when faced with wicked problems.

In her article, 'Could you be a "Super Forecaster"?', Tara Isabella Burton (2015) summarises the findings of The Good Judgement Project that people from 'ordinary walks of life' are routinely far better at predicting events than experts.

Tetlock and his team discovered a group of 'super forecasters' who had similar personality traits rather than specialised knowledge. The reasons for their success have been described as 'open-minded thinking'. One of the super forecasters described his talent as being 'active open-minded thinking' and another as 'not addressing any question with any particular attachment' or viewpoint he was hoping to prove or disprove.

In her article, Burton describes the super forecasters for that year as being a diverse group, including finance workers, an oil painter, an animator and a factory machine maker. The study involved two different groups who were asked to predict the outcomes of specific scenarios.

One group was made up of random people from all walks of life, the other of intelligence analysts well versed in the fields they were asked to interpret – even being given access to confidential information to help them. The results were astonishing, as time and again it proved to be the random group who were more accurate in their interpretations and predictions.

This isn't to denigrate expertise and experience; merely to underline the fact that we all need to think beyond our boundaries and delve beneath our assumptions to discover new ways of working and learning.

The scavenger mindset manages to navigate complexity by creating a growth environment. The concern isn't to be 'right', but to learn and bring the very best of what we have to meet the goals we share.

Scavenger is not as alien a concept as it might

appear. Consider the times you've had to adapt plans quickly when an unexpected situation arose, or when you needed to make the most of a situation despite not having the ideal surroundings or tools for the job.

All of these are the signs of resourcefulness, enterprise and creativity that make you a scavenger leader – and this is what we need now more than ever.

Scavenger pioneer #1

Louise Goulden, The Together Project

It's not always wise to meet your heroes: too often the reality doesn't live up to the expectation. But meeting scavenger leaders who are pioneers in their field is a completely different experience, as the human element is wonderfully apparent in every aspect of their stories. They represent a dynamic mix of determination, ingenuity, courage and optimism.

Louise Goulden's award-winning The Together Project exemplifies the scavenger approach. I first met Louise on a dark, wet December morning in a steamed-up coffee shop in Walthamstow, north London. I was fascinated to learn about her journey from highly successful marketeer to founder of a successful grassroots company, via the stepping-stone of motherhood. True to all the scavenger pioneers, she's open, engaging and energising, and totally surprised by the incredible success her project has already achieved.

Louise launched a movement which has connected

people at either end of the life-stage spectrum, and found real harmony there. Her decision to set up The Together Project was a big leap of faith but, after having her baby, she found she wanted more than her previous career had offered: a role that could make a tangible difference, and would allow her to work from home.

As it turned out, her answer lay close by. Taking her son to meet an elderly relative in a care home, she was fascinated by the natural rapport between them: it left Louise feeling as if she'd witnessed something simple but profound. This discovery sparked an idea to create a mothers' and toddlers' music group based in, and including, the elderly in their care homes. And so the seeds of The Together Project were sown.

The brilliance of the idea is in its simplicity and the immediacy of its value. Carefully crafted sessions meet the needs of all involved, providing stimulus and flow through the medium of music and song. The children, the elderly and all the adults involved find something of real joy and value in this transaction. Louise has seen first-hand the extraordinary transformation which can result from bringing children and their parents into care homes, where the elderly are frequently left to their own devices.

Louise's enterprise heralds a new level of empathy and understanding between the generations. She has shown how we can all benefit from small interactions that end up helping the givers as much as the receivers. Like many of us, Louise has always strived for perfection, worrying about details, but one of her biggest lessons has been to learn to accept 'good enough' as a standard. She admits that this is far more effective in moving things forward and creating the space for learning.

We can all benefit from letting go of perfection to allow space for innovation. Sometimes, tinkering and reshaping are more about our fear of action than a demand for the ideal.

3 Scavenger leadership: from grassroots to the boardroom

The scourers

The scavenger mindset shows up most clearly in those leaders who, like me, began with nothing, but unlike me, went on to grow their initiative into a mighty, impactful organisation. The scavenger pioneers scattered throughout this book are examples of scourers: leaders whom I first met a couple of years ago, and who inspired me greatly. You can find scourers everywhere: leaders who have seemingly come from nowhere, yet brought people together to achieve something incredible. They scour the landscape for resources and people to help them meet their goal, demonstrating high levels of enterprise and resourcefulness.

Psychologist Sara Sarasrathy (2008) researched the essential qualities of successful 'scavenger' entrepreneurs, referring to them as 'effectually minded people'. She points to their ability to consider the tools and materials at their disposal, and a 'springboard for envisioning what new directions they can take', as some of the key reasons for their success.

How often do you look at what you have and wish you had better skills or were better equipped? Scourers work with what they have, and make it work really well. They prove that all too often we make assumptions about someone's abilities and capacity to contribute. With the right conditions, anyone is capable of far more than we imagine, including ourselves. These leaders have lessons for all of us on how to really motivate people and lead in such a way that brings out the best in everyone.

On the surface, scourers may not appear to be obvious leadership material, as few carry the credentials we associate with leadership. Many don't have the 'right' qualifications, background or experience; but they're ideally placed to tackle wicked problems, as they hold few preconceived ideas and work hard at actively engaging people in learning about the best direction to take, and then take it.

How they manage to achieve this is by starting small and simple.

- Pamela Warhurst (scavenger pioneer #2) talks about how her first goal was to 'start as many conversations as possible'.
- Adam Smith (scavenger pioneer #3) sent out

5,000 emails, but began with just two responses.

- Sophia Parker (scavenger pioneer #4) began by asking parents a question: 'Does anyone else feel the same as I do about throwing away so much baby paraphernalia?'

We sometimes rail against anything that seems too simple, but simplicity is precisely why it's so powerful. Again, Pamela summed it up beautifully when she said:

What we needed wasn't strategy documents and committee meetings, but something really simple that would enable a whole community to live their lives differently. (Warhurst and Dobson 2014)

When I worked on other high-street regeneration projects, all too often the temptation was to fill in the spaces where uncertainty lurked. There was a deep-rooted reluctance to let the learning curve take care of itself. In my experience, wrapping the learning around everyone as the project progresses ensures building strong community resilience.

In *The Abundant Community*, John McKnight sums up the key elements of developing community around a project or challenge: 'The community development approach begins with connecting people to their own internal personal resources [, skills] and community resources to effect change' (McKnight and Block 2010).

This is what each scavenger leader instinctively

achieves, building trust throughout the process. Trust doesn't exist in a vacuum; it grows when people feel respected. Adam Smith's approach to leadership was to trust his team's judgement and ability to decide how to behave, with his one rule of 'Don't be a dick' (later amended to 'Be Kind'). In a wicked world there isn't time to control every action, or monitor every result.

Scourers demonstrate extraordinary perseverance, capitalising on the freedom their clean slate affords them. If they didn't feel they had adequate resources, many people would give up before they started. My own experience of attracting two people to that first meeting on my local high street, or Adam Smith receiving two responses to the 5,000 emails he sent out, might well have been the sign-off point for many – but our perseverance and belief in our aims paid off.

Another of my scavenger inspirations is Jane Addams (see Chapter 8). In her book *20 Years at Hull House* (1910), she wrote about her experience of setting up a community space for immigrant communities in Chicago in the 1900s. She typifies the scourer: 'In those days we made no appeal for money, meaning to start with our slender resources.' Despite a number of setbacks, Hull House became a vital community space that transformed lives.

Leaders like this aren't deterred by having nothing. They dig deeper to understand where the viable opportunities and real challenges lie.

Scourers know they need the support and participation of others, and that this can take time. Pamela Warhurst had worked for the government, and was clear about the differences in her approach:

> It's not like a government programme that always has a beginning, middle and end. It's all about inputs and outputs and thousands of tiny steps that build trust over long periods. (Warhurst and Dobson 2014)

This may sound onerous, but no matter the size or scale of the project, investing in tiny, powerful steps is what leads to the greatest long-term success. Not only do these scourers have to attract people to work alongside them; but they also need to provide an environment in which those people can thrive. Their leadership style is necessarily collaborative, and they're able to create highly effective teams from completely random groups of people. They have a clear sense of direction, but are open to the route they take to get there. Without the benefit of a human resources department or CV selection process, they look beyond the boundaries of what we generally expect from people. Through an 'all hands on deck' approach, they show that with the right conditions in place, people of all kinds are capable of far more than our conventional approach to leadership suggests. They equip people to work together productively by focusing on what matters most, and motivate people by valuing their involvement and cultivating a sense of ownership.

The Friendship Bench

In his book *Creative Blindness (And How to Cure It)* (2019), Dave Trott refers to an extraordinary example in Zimbabwe.

Dixon Chibanda was one of only 12 psychiatrists in a country of 14 million people. Following a tragic incident where a young woman took her own life, Dixon decided that he needed to find a creative solution to the problem. There were grandmothers in every village, so his solution was to start training grandmothers in basic cognitive behavioural therapy, where the patient and the practitioner solved the problem together.

Dixon created the Friendship Bench – an open-air wooden bench where a young woman could talk to a grandmother. Hundreds of grandmothers have now treated 70,000 patients, and young women in that country are five times less likely to have suicidal thoughts.

How simple but effective – what does this brilliant idea tell you about how much more can be achieved if we start to think differently about where opportunity, ownership and value lie?

Scourers have important lessons for us all about the value of understanding what really motivates people, and recognising that the level of someone's contribution is a direct reflection of how they feel. The most unlikely people can have the most important insights. Scourers challenge what it takes to be a successful leader. They're able to build highly effective communities, and often exceed their intended goal. With little or no experience, money, resources or infrastructure, they defy expectations and break through limiting beliefs. They master uncertainty, learn to dance with complexity and demonstrate that everyone performs better when we can let our goal guide, but not divide, us.

What we see most of all through the filter of these high-achieving individuals are qualities that, in fact, exist in us all.

The boardroom beauties

Contrary to what the name might suggest, scavenger leaders can be found in some of the most conventional organisations.

These boardroom beauties shine a light on how the scavenger mindset can work anywhere and benefit every type of leader. They need courage, conviction and imagination in the same amounts as those that begin with nothing. They may already have the resources and the framework, but that in itself is a challenge. For these more established leaders, the dilemma is how to achieve a mindset shift in an environment where people may be anxious about change, wedded to an established way of doing things, and decisiveness is highly valued.

Recent events, from the financial crash to the pandemic, have resulted in high levels of uncertainty, and heralded a universal recognition of wicked-style problems, creating the groundwork for more receptive responses to the scavenger mindset and leadership style.

The absolute master of this was Dee Hock, the trailblazer CEO of Visa, whose vision was to create a universal currency that transcended national boundaries. Hock described Visa as an 'enabling organisation' – living proof that a large company can be highly effective without being centralised or coercive: it could be argued that Visa was successful precisely because it wasn't either of these.

As Hock said:

> It was beyond the power of reason to design an organisation to deal with such worldwide complexity… and beyond the power of imagination to perceive all the conditions encountered. (Mitchell Waldrop 1996)

The only viable solution was to devise a system that allowed its members to create their own price and market, and to service their product under the Visa umbrella – creating a blend of competition and cooperation. (For more about Hock, see Chapter 8.)

Peter Senge, author of *The Fifth Discipline* (2006), sets out how to create a learning organisation, and the benefits of achieving this:

> In situations of rapid change, only those that are flexible, adaptive and productive will excel. For

this to happen... organisations need to discover how to tap people's commitment and capacity to learn at all levels.

Senge underlines how leaders must now enrol the full range of people within an organisation so as to learn quickly, effectively and capture the full potential within. Similarly, an article about learning organisations on the MBA knowledge website mentions 'boundaryless organisations' that learn and apply that learning, and 'may be the only sustainable source of competitive edge'.

The article also references IBM under the leadership of Lou Gerstner, whose outsider status caused controversy when he was first appointed CEO. He brought the technology giant back from the brink of bankruptcy, and fundamentally changed the company culture from one of unhealthy levels of competition between teams to one where it was possible to build stronger collaborations and cooperation between teams.

The issue is how to 'safely' introduce an approach that's upfront about doubt into a world that expects certainty and demands control. All true scavenger leaders understand the significance of uncertainty, the opportunity it affords in terms of innovation and the competitive edge it creates. But leaders need to do some unlearning about what's really required when dealing with wicked problems.

The challenge is how to create space, metaphorically and physically, within a conventional approach that allows this new mindset to emerge. It isn't something that can be helicoptered into an organisation; rather, a process of self-learning where small step-change is vital, and a deep dive into what's really happening is essential.

This mindset represents a big shift for many people, but small changes grow confidence and produce evidence of success. To the scavenger leader, learning to accept and master uncertainty, face conflict and address areas of challenge are vital when it comes to building a sustainable approach to success.

Sara Sarasrathy's (2008) study showed that entrepreneurs were successful not through goal-setting or having a big vision to follow; rather, the ability to adopt an 'unconventional' approach to learning, namely 'an improvisational flexibility... and a willingness to change direction'. Our organisational systems have developed a reliance on measuring outcomes and inputs in a specific way, as well as evaluating performance to give credence and weight to decisions and plans. Anything that runs counter to that needs to be introduced with care, and with an approach that brings people with you, being mindful of how uncomfortable it might first appear.

Ultimately this is about learning to work with reality instead of simply trying to control it.

Why trying to control reality won't work in a wicked world

Ever since the collapse of Enron in 2001, there has been a growing catalogue of disasters in organisations where the leadership has come unstuck by trying to control reality rather than working with it. The need to be in control, expect neat answers and to be proven right has steered some leaders into troubled waters, creating a climate of fear that prevents the reality of a situation from being properly acknowledged and addressed.

The decline of Nokia

Infamously, in the space of just six years, Nokia went from being a globally dominant, innovative technology giant with the bestselling mobile brand to losing 90 per cent of its market. It's a cautionary tale about what can go wrong, and even the most successful of companies can be destabilised.

For years, Nokia had switched off its thinking about a fast-changing market and its dynamic competition. In a study published in 2015, Timo Vuori, a professor at Aalto University in Helsinki, blamed the culture of fear that permeated the organisation as the main reason for the company's downfall (Vuori and Huy 2015). Top executives were frightened of admitting to themselves, customers and suppliers that their technology was inferior to Apple's. Middle managers,

71

fearful of losing their jobs if they told the truth to senior managers, told the emperor his clothes looked amazing, while knowing only too well he was naked.

The article stated that one way to avoid this being repeated was an ability and power to challenge and question the status quo, and that this is the 'only way that leaders can address and manage change' (Vuori and Huy 2015). For many organisations, this is easier said than done, requiring a level of safety that would echo South Africa's truth and reconciliation model – but well worth the effort.

Boardroom beauties understand the value of granting permission to challenge and question. How else can they learn and stay effective? If people are afraid to be open and reluctant to challenge or offer alternative viewpoints, the organisation is in danger of extinction.

The delusion of Theranos

The downfall of Theranos, an American start-up launched by Elizabeth Holmes, is well documented (e.g. Carreyrou 2018). It promised a new system of diagnosing multiple health problems from a small drop of blood.

The idea was brilliant, and many people wanted so much to believe it could be done, that they ignored the warning signs. Holmes attracted millions in investment and support from some of the most eminent leaders in the USA.

The problem was that despite huge investment, it just wasn't possible. Aside from the sheer audacity of promoting a health solution that was no more than an idea, and despite many staff members raising concerns, the illusion of success was allowed to grow over many years.

Holmes raises many questions for us all: what was her motivation, and how did so many people fall under her spell and allow so much pretence to go unchallenged?

A similar story unfolded inside WeWork, founded by the charismatic Adam Neumann and once valued at $47bn. *Wall Street Journal* correspondent Eliot Brown described the company as 'A $20bn Start-up Fueled by Silicon Valley Pixie Dust' (quoted in Zeitlin 2019).

Both of these contemporary tales have been made into TV series and, like modern-day fables, they stand as warnings that just because a leader says so, doesn't mean to say they're right or should be blindly followed. In wicked times, it's unhealthy to have a leader who is unwilling to be challenged, questioned, unable to adapt or pivot – or indeed one that blinds others with their charisma.

This situation is not confined to the private sector. There have been examples in the charitable sector too, with scandals hitting The Red Cross, Save the Children and Oxfam (Elliot and Sullivan 2015; O'Neill 2018; Campbell 2018). Reports of a 'collective failure of leadership' in this sector as well as the public sector led to toxic work environments and disastrous outcomes. In his report on the Liverpool Community Health NHS Trust scandal, Dr Bill Kirkup described that with 'an oppressive culture pursuing unrealistic financial goals, an organisation can quickly mutate into one that harms the very people it is there to serve' (Kirkup 2018).

In each case, blind adherence to a strategy that involved overambitious targets created a climate of fear and mistrust that, in effect, disabled the organisations and were the cause of traumatic mistakes. Fear is an inhibitor on every level and never produces great results. What is clear is that whatever the type of organisation or community, trying to squeeze wicked problems into tame boxes results in devastating outcomes.

The ongoing example is, of course, the pandemic, and the emerging picture of how different leaders have tried to show authority in the face of such devastation and flux.

Mismanaging the pandemic

From the beginning, the British Government's response was straight out of the conventional leadership textbook: ministers tried to maintain control by issuing one ambitious target after another: personal protective equipment (PPE), then Test and Trace, which, when it failed to materialise, undermined the government's authority and people's trust in leaders. At a time when this was critical, it was catastrophic, only to be over-shadowed by later revelations of indiscreet revelry.

Once the narrative had been set, there seemed little opportunity to pause, reflect and consider what was actually within their power to deliver, and therefore what mattered most. Scientists warned that Covid-19 was likely to be unpredictable, but despite asserting that the government was heeding their advice, this wasn't always evident.

Sadly, it's a demonstration of leadership that doesn't really understand how to lead through wicked times. A scavenger leader would have come up with a narrative that was upfront about uncertainty and acknowledged limitations but communicated a deter-mination to evolve a strategy in line with scientific data. Focusing on what they did know, what could be achieved and utilising resources that did exist, they could have pulled together key stakeholders and built partnerships – whatever the colour of their politics.

When we look at all our major institutions and organisations, the majority of them would benefit from an injection of the scavenger mindset to shake up their boundaries and reimagine their futures. In wicked times, leadership isn't about finding answers; it's about collective engagement and widening the scope of understanding. Scavenger leaders are best placed to adapt, change and build community around their ideas. No one should be excluded or underesti-mated here – young, old, educated, uneducated. Strip away the boxes and the neat labels, and we can all have important contributions to make and valid insights to share.

As the world's resources become scarcer, new approaches to leadership are emerging. There are increasing examples of scavenger-style leadership in all walks of life – and scavenger leaders make it their business not only to know where the influence lies, but how to use it.

Scavenger success stories

There are already signs of positive change. Iceland now has an all-female cabinet, and the Prime Minister of New Zealand, Jacinda Ardern, has won high praise and respect around the world for her clear-sighted, compassionate leadership. Most recently, the brilliant President of Ukraine, Volodymyr Zelenskyy, has demonstrated a calibre of leadership which has yet to be attained by the Eton brigade.

In local UK politics, Preston and Wigan are evolving new ways of working, and the Participatory City initiative offers a collaborative approach to building sustainable communities, with wellbeing and equality at their centre. And after being sickened by the plastic she saw in the sea during her solo voyage around the world, the international sailor Dame Ellen MacArthur created a foundation to support and promote the circular economy, encouraging businesses to actively consider how to be successful while being mindful of their impact on the world.

A great example of this is the Green Salon Collective, an organisation that recycles a variety of waste from hair salons throughout the UK and Ireland: human hair has been put to good use as an effective absorber of oil spills in the sea. Businesses have been rethinking how they operate based on what they value. The millennial generation places huge value on organisational responsibility and green credentials.

Even in the most conventional companies there are examples of radical rethinking. Jack Welch, former chair and CEO of General Electric, advocated bound-aryless organisations to find ways to surface potential, knowledge and insights that may otherwise have remained dormant in departments.

Over recent years, an increasing number of corporate global leaders have looked again and deeper at their operating models to reimagine how they could work more effectively in a changing world. Big brands such as Google, Apple, Nike, Levi's and Renault have reflected external changes in consumer power, and understand that sustainability is critical. The circular economy, collaborative consumption and C2C (cradle-to-cradle) are all emerging models that focus on using resources in a more sparing and innovative way.

Organisations that have given responsibility to people throughout the business have seen shifts in performance that reflect the trust placed in them. In his book *Reinventing Organizations*, Frederic Laloux (2014) introduces the idea of 'teal' organisations that shun conventional work structures, and are proving how much people can achieve together when a more collaborative approach is taken. Leaders are less 'in control', and more 'in support'.

In each of the examples that follow, these companies have adopted an approach to meeting goals that beautifully reflect the scavenger mindset. They have achieved amazing results in not only motivating people, but also in improving their financial results.

Intuit: software designed with the user in mind

Intuit is a financial software company founded by Scott Cook, designed to make managing finances easier for individuals and businesses. Cook was inspired to launch Intuit when his wife complained about how time-consuming and tedious the job of managing household finances had become. It seemed to Cook that this was likely to be a universal issue – one that could be addressed by technology.

He decided to do some research on the scope of the problem. He visited his local library and used a phone book to call households in the area to determine what problems they faced with their personal financial management. He discovered that his wife was indeed representative of most of the people he spoke to, but that there were already a couple of dozen software products on the market.

After talking to users of the market leader, Cook realised it was too complicated to operate: only 4 per cent of people who had bought it were actually using it. Scott's focus on continually engaging customers to discover what worked and what didn't has been one of the main reasons for Intuit's phenomenal success. Intuit consistently tests its products on users to make sure it doesn't make assumptions about what works.

This high level of active engagement, delving beneath assumptions to understand what's really going on, propelled Intuit's business to a 94 per cent share of the market – and it remains consistently at the top of its field.

What mattered most: doing the groundwork and challenging assumptions.

Interface: saving the planet, one carpet at a time

Ray Anderson, the pioneering CEO of US-based company Interface, put sustainability front and centre of his agenda way back in the early 1990s. It began when he was asked a question that he was unable to answer: 'What's your company doing for the environment?'

The resulting work was transformational. The question of how to become more sustainable ignited innovation throughout the organisation, and saw immediate results on the bottom line. Reusing materials cut costs, and eliminating toxic waste eliminated disposal costs. Everyone in the company was involved in thinking about how Interface might become environmentally sustainable.

In doing so, Anderson increased productivity and profits, while having a hugely positive impact on the environment. When he started on this journey, he didn't know exactly what being sustainable might look like, and had to convince the board and shareholders of the value of this approach. What he couldn't have anticipated was how the entire organisation would start thinking about how it could support this aim, and what might be done to achieve it.

One of the extraordinary results of this innovative new thinking was Net-Works, a collaboration with the Zoological Society of London, that recycles wasted fishing nets from some of the poorest communities in the world, providing them with new income and reducing waste, protecting ocean ecosystems and marine life.

What mattered most: sustainability.

Rowe Furniture: from conveyor belts to collaboration

Back in 1995, Charlene Pedrolie, the newly appointed manufacturing chief of US company Rowe Furniture, was tasked with creating a hyper-efficient assembly process.

For decades, Rowe's factory had run in a robotic

way, with individuals performing the same function day after day. Whatever the board had been expecting, it probably wasn't Charlene inviting everyone on the factory floor to redesign a better, more efficient system. The process was a long one of learning, testing, trying and failing and, had it not been for Charlene's belief, it might have ended prematurely.

As Thomas Petzinger (1999) reflects in his book *The New Pioneers*, after 'several weeks of plant-wide pandemonium the pieces at last fell into place, causing productivity and quality to shoot through the roof'. The collective intelligence and insights revealed through this exercise resulted in a team-based production process, designed and run by the people closest to the action. Petzinger (1999) describes the Rowe Furniture turnaround as revealing:

> the creative power of human interaction. It suggests that efficiency is intrinsic, and that people are naturally productive when inspired by a vision, equipped with the right tools.

What mattered most: being more productive through collective intelligence and design.

Buurtzorg Nederland: healthcare in the community begins with the patient

As a community nurse in the Netherlands, Jos de Blok found his work was becoming increasingly spreadsheet centred. His visits to clients were timed and his day scheduled by head office, with a focus on efficiency.

Jos became increasingly frustrated with this approach. Clients were glanced over rather than properly cared for, and for Jos this was a travesty. As a result, he set up Buurtzorg Nederland with just ten nurses and one rule: to spend a minimum of 11 minutes with each client. This allowed clients to feel valued, and gave the nurses an opportunity not only to appraise their situation, but also to build relationships.

In doing so, they discovered other informal support networks that their clients could call on if necessary. In setting up this new organisation, the nurses were given training to run their own service, and there was no longer a central command making poorly informed decisions. The leaders' role was to offer support and guidance, but not to step in – and never to take control.

The results were astounding. Even though Buurtzorg nurses are more expensive, they save time and money in the long run. Clients recover better, become more independent and, if they go to hospital, they spend less time there. An Ernst & Young study in 2009 found that Buurtzorg requires on average 40 per cent fewer hours of care than other nursing organisations, and that the savings for the Dutch social security system would be close to €2 billion if all home care organisations achieved Buurtzorg results (Laloux 2014).

What mattered most: client autonomy.

Scavenger pioneer #2

Pamela Warhurst, Incredible Edible

'We weren't going to wait for permission, and we certainly weren't going to wait for anyone to give us money.'

Pamela is the founder of the hugely successful Incredible Edible movement, which has inspired thousands of people to transform their communities into collaborative, connected, kinder places through the medium of food. Set up in 2007, there are now more than 100 Incredible Edibles in the UK, and more than 1,000 worldwide.

I first met Pamela in a quiet hotel in Leeds, and was excited to meet someone I admired as a social innovator and grassroots icon. Pamela is a slight woman who might pass unnoticed in the street – but when she talks, you listen. Her keen intelligence is fuelled by exasperation, and her innate sense of responsibility makes her narrative compelling. She tells her story straight from her heart with wit and wisdom, underscored by credentials and achievements that most Fortune 500 companies would love to boast about.

Pamela explained that Incredible Edible's beginnings were a direct response to an overwhelming sense of frustration at the lack of meaningful change achieved through a top-down approach to climate change. As she attended yet another climate change conference, it seemed to her that nothing would ever shift.

Pamela was motivated to take action, and sketched

out a community-led response on the back of a napkin. Her genius was to identify, within the chaos of climate complexity, a small step-change that could engage people at a simple, accessible point: food.

She took her idea to her friend, Mary Clear, and they spent the night shaping Pamela's idea into a vision, identifying small actions that could begin the process of change. With no funds, resources or template, together they came up with the idea of using wasted public realm to start growing vegetables, and inviting people to take them home to cook and eat.

This simple idea began to capture people's imagination. One day, Mary found a casserole dish containing vegetable soup on her doorstep, left by a grateful mother who had made good use of the vegetables and herbs, and wanted to say thank you.

Growing, giving, cooking, eating and sharing food brought a community together, and inspired a myriad of related initiatives involving the wide-ranging needs and skills of the community.

Pamela's passion stems from her family and community, as well as a steely determination to reverse the effects of climate change at community level.

Incredible Edible is a perfect example of just how much people are capable of, given the right impetus and conditions. Pamela would readily admit that while she's the inspiration and architect, others have brought her vision to life and made Incredible Edible the success it is today. There have been challenges, but the grassroots approach not only allows for these but expects them, so it's able to address issues head-on, as and when they occur.

As the movement grows, Pamela is insistent that it's 'scaling up' and 'spreading'. This is a subtle but important difference that alludes to the power of a scavenger approach: understanding the potential in others to meet their own challenges, and deliver success when given the right motivation and support to do so.

Ultimately, the scavenger approach is about getting results.

4 Lessons from scavenger leaders

As we've seen, scavenger leaders are able to embrace uncertainty, build strong, relationship-based communities, stimulate critical and creative thinking and provide an ideal environment for innovation.

This may feel like a leap outside your comfort zone, but remember that the scavenger mindset isn't another framework or model – it leads to a process of learning that is both respectful and mindful of organisational context, and designed to work for anyone.

The only requirement of the scavenger mindset is a belief in, or curiosity about, the untapped capabilities and skills of any team, anywhere – and the job of a scavenger leader is to build from that. According to Keith Grint, the reason that 75 per cent of change initiatives fail is that too often the process of change is mistaken for restructuring (Grint and Holt 2011). The scavenger mindset isn't about starting again from scratch or introducing some new and shiny initiative. As mentioned previously, it's about understanding what you actually have and working better with it.

Each example of scavenger leadership in this book demonstrates the following five lessons:

1. You *never* have nothing – start small, but start somewhere.
2. Ask questions to build community.
3. Big is rarely better.
4. Not knowing is a superpower.
5. Let go of perfect.

1. You *never* have nothing – start small, but start somewhere

Even if you're sitting on your own at your desk with nothing but pencil and paper, you never have nothing. Everything in your lived experience indicates evidence of your ability to adapt, learn and survive.

Consider your network and what experience, skills and contacts they might offer, from family, neighbours and colleagues to friends and acquaintances. As all the scavenger pioneers in this book demonstrate, you only need one person to start something, and with social media, finding people is easier than ever.

In established organisations, there will always be people who may have been overlooked, not involved or simply under the radar. There is a rich source of inspiration and ideas all around you.

Would you:

- Give a job to a young school dropout without any qualifications to their name?
- Hire a pensioner to run your global teams?
- Expect a nurse to design a better healthcare system than a CEO?
- Expect a community to find a way to reinvent itself?

As we've seen previously, we've been brought up to believe that qualifications and experience are key to the contribution we're able to make. This is a belief that scavenger leaders challenge and demonstrate that, with the right approach, people from all walks of life can contribute in meaningful ways. Pamela Warhurst is passionate in her belief that 'people are magnificent'. In his book *Everybody Matters*, Bob Chapman, CEO of Barry-Wehmiller, says it loud and clear: 'The truth is that talent of all kinds is lurking in our organisations… people are fine, it's our leadership that's lacking' (Chapman and Sisodia 2015).

- What are the beliefs you hold around what people are capable of, and where their potential really lies?
- What do you rely on to gauge someone's suitability?

The scavenger leaders introduced here are all remarkable people who have achieved extraordinary results. This in itself is impressive, but what is even more so is that they achieved their goals by working with disparate groups of people who formed highly effective teams. They worked with whoever walked through the door, and did so with welcoming arms.

There will always be people we know or work with who can offer help or insight – but they may not be our normal 'go-to' people. Take a leaf out of the scavenger handbook and look beyond the title, role or level of experience.

Ideas and support can come from the least likely people, so don't discount anyone. Challenge your assumptions!

Scavenger questions

- What are the credentials or qualifications you consider to be non-negotiable?
- What are the most important qualities you look for in someone with whom you want to work?
- How much are you missing by only looking at a CV?

2. Ask questions to build community

No matter what their scale, complex problems require people to come together and bring a wide range of insights and questions to the table. Asking questions helps to drive collaboration, learning and innovation.

A question can become a navigation tool that keeps everyone on track.

Interface boss Ray Anderson's question about how his company could become sustainable (see Chapter 3) ran in tandem with the rest of the business, and elicited wide-ranging interest that proved to be a powerful way to motivate and connect people.

My aim of improving the footfall and value of the high street began with a basic question about what value the high street actually had, and how it could be regenerated locally.

Pamela Warhurst's question for her initiative was: 'What could connect the community and help them to explore ways of becoming self-sufficient?'

Adam Smith's question was: 'How do we stop food going to waste and redistribute it to where need is greatest?'

It's about beginning with big-picture questions that draw out new ideas and allow the details to emerge as more is learned and understood. This 'Pied Piper' question needs to call out to everyone, bringing together a diversity of voices. The emphasis needs to be on creating a community of learning, with a clear point of connection established early on that can gloss over any superficial divisions.

Communities only work if time is spent on building relationships over and above any roles or titles. Communication needs to be open and free-flowing, so that people are properly furnished with relevant information, and have clear operational guidelines that allow for meaningful contributions.

Scavenger questions

- How can you turn your goal into a question?
- Which perspective is missing?
- What will success look like, and how will you celebrate?

3. Big is rarely better

If they're not seen as viable or relevant, big budgets and ambitious outcomes can be demotivating: they can feel overwhelming, debilitating and unrealistic.

The big budgets of high-street regeneration projects seem to stifle people rather than motivate them. Small starts give greater freedom: with less to lose, you can afford to be more open and generous in your attitude. They're explicitly about learning, so building in a process where people can reflect, review and reframe is important.

As scavenger leaders know, however small the start, it creates energy, gives focus and attracts attention from others. Small starts lend themselves to sustainable growth and the likelihood of greater success, giving an opportunity to think more creatively. They might mean working with no extra resources or budgets, but they can be the key to unlocking fresh thinking and more courageous contributions.

When asking a scavenger question, there may be no specific answer or end point, but it will generate insights that need to be captured and contextualised:

- ◆ What have we learned?
- ◆ What does that tell us?
- ◆ What do we need to change?

Just like the game of snakes and ladders, there will be outcomes that work, and others where the outcome teaches us something important. What may look like a snake – i.e. a failure in small-start learning environments – can reveal new information and fresh insights.

'Possible' doesn't necessarily mean 'do it'

One of my own 'snake' moments was when a basic loyalty card was introduced into the high street regeneration project.

On paper, it looked like the perfect idea: we had built a real community connection, and it seemed a great way to build on that. While the card went down well with the community, it failed to achieve the results we'd hoped for, as we simply hadn't made the case for its value to the participating businesses. Too many businesses would only offer the loyalty reward if they were expressly asked for it by their customers!

The lesson I learned here was to keep a check on my assumptions: that just because something was possible, didn't mean it should be done.

Scavenger questions

* How might starting small make life easier for you?
* What are the challenges of starting small, and how do you know that to be true?
* Where are you being too big?

4. Not knowing is a superpower

If you look ahead to the next six to 12 months, how much of what you're planning now can you be confident will come to fruition in exactly the way you're currently envisioning?

Life has always been in a state of constant flux, but now we need to embrace this rather than trying to deny it. As this book illustrates, my whole life has been an admission that I don't know, but that has never stopped me from acting and learning. I'd argue that had I been confident about my future plans, I may well have been tempted to switch off my thinking and become complacent.

Not knowing places us in an actively engaged learning state. Increasingly, 'I don't know' is the only honest response. And during the pandemic, we've shown ourselves to be far more capable of agile, adaptable, independent leadership than ever before.

I believe this is no aberration. We've all experienced huge amounts of change and uncertainty, and lived to tell the tale. We've survived not knowing. We're built for it, we've lived it and mastered it. Now we need to reconnect with the opportunities that exist in challenging times.

Scavenger leaders are scanners. They're constantly on the lookout for emerging problems and opportunities, scanning the horizon to identify where action is needed, and what needs to be learned in order to progress. They take nothing for granted, and keep an open mind; they gain expertise through involvement, and broaden their perspective by listening to different people.

Dynamic and determined, scavenger leaders are able to dive through the waves of change, assessing the best routes to their goal based on the context they're in and the resources they have. The beauty of not knowing is that it pushes us to learn and imagine. Not knowing becomes your superpower to knock down complacency and introduce switched-on thinking. You need to rebrand doubt as the trigger for valuable learning and growth.

Scavenger questions

◆ What don't you know?
◆ What happens when things don't go according to plan?
◆ What is the most important thing to find out?

5. Let go of perfect

There are occasions when perfect is perfectly acceptable: for example, the chef who values precision and wants to create the 'perfect' plate of food; the orchestra playing a note-perfect symphony or the surgeon perfecting the art of surgery.

However, when it comes to leadership in uncertain times, perfection is neither useful nor relevant. Letting go of perfect isn't about saying farewell to your best friend. It's more about saying goodbye to the mean friend: the one that constantly brings you down, stops you from taking part and makes you feel 'less-than'.

Embracing imperfection

The Japanese have the right idea when it comes to understanding perfection. *Kintsugi* is the art of repairing broken pottery by piecing it back together with lacquer mixed with powdered gold, silver or platinum. It's built on the idea that, in embracing flaws and imperfections, you can create an even stronger, more beautiful piece of art. Every break is unique, and the 400-year-old technique actually highlights the 'scars' as part of the design.

Using this as a metaphor for healing ourselves teaches us an important lesson: sometimes in the process of repairing things that have broken, we actually create something more unique and resilient. This is a lovely idea to hold on to, and to encourage a culture that sees value in imperfection.

I understand that letting go might sound frightening. It suggests a loss of control, rather like falling without a parachute. But it's actually about letting go of that which no longer serves us or is stopping us from moving forward. From mindsets to meetings, you need to consider what might be holding you back, and seek to change it.

Let go of the *illusion* of perfection and your obsession with achieving it. For a scavenger leader, this means using your time more effectively and allowing others to take greater responsibility, even to do things their way rather than yours. The community organiser Saul Alinsky (1971) believed that unless people felt they had real power in decisions and processes, they would never contribute more than their bare minimum. Any reluctance to allow people greater ownership may stem from fear of letting go of authority.

Over the years, I've learned that trying to maintain the illusion of perfection is idiotic. Even in the Instagram era, no one really believes in perfect. There's truth in the saying that a problem shared is a problem halved – and divulging the full picture, with the good news and the bad, helps to build a sense of community. There is a benefit in 'facing the uglies': facing up to reality and addressing issues as they arise in a spirit of intelligent curiosity, honesty and kindness.

We're all fallible. It's one of those simple human truths that, once admitted, creates an environment where we can accept mistakes and find solutions. If you don't expect perfection in others, you're more able to accept your own flaws – which strengthens your ability to withstand problems when things don't go according to plan. As Louise Goulden discovered, it was only when she let go of the reins and her expectation that everything had to be 'perfect' that she made progress. In wicked scenarios, there is no time or place for perfection, and it probably doesn't exist anyway.

Seeking perfection may be habitual, but in my experience, it can become the acceptable face of procrastination.

Scavenger questions

◆ What are you holding on to that no longer serves?

◆ Where is perfection preventing progression?

◆ How might letting go of perfect benefit the people with whom you live or work?

Scavenger pioneer #3

Adam Smith, The Real Junk Food Project

'We worked with whoever walked through the door.'

Adam Smith launched The Real Junk Food Project in 2013. Within five years it had intercepted 5,000 tonnes of discarded food, creating 11.9 million meals. This community interest company has won multiple awards and is growing by the day, encouraging hundreds of people to start Project cafes, projects and social supermarkets, helping to feed the world, change behaviours and save food that otherwise would have gone to waste.

It could be said that Wakefield-based Adam personifies the Northern Powerhouse, as he is one of the most extraordinary and highly effective individuals I've ever met. With true-grit drive and overwhelming energy, if his spirit were bottled, the UK would now be taking the lead and inspiring others to achieve more with less.

Like all scavenger pioneer journeys, Adam's started from small beginnings and with a razor-sharp vision. His ideas weren't shaped in committee meetings or conference halls, or planned around a brief or budget. Despite his clear vision, there was no detailed plan about *how* it would be achieved, just a determination that it *should* be.

Adam had trained as a chef, and it was while working on a farm in Australia that he saw first-hand the vast amounts of food going to waste. The absurdity of it, the evidence of growing need and the inspiration of local cafes that were serving recycled food, helped him form the idea for the Project. The truth was that people weren't going hungry because there wasn't enough food; it was simply a matter of distribution.

As this book has identified, scavenger pioneers have to work with whatever resources are available, and find a way to make the most of them. This makes them incredibly agile, resourceful and effective, and Adam is a perfect example of that. Having come up with the concept for the Project, Adam sent out 5,000 emails to various organisations and individuals that he felt would be interested in his vision.

His journey began after receiving just two replies. The first of his 'Pay As You Feel' cafes was launched in Armley, Leeds, has now fed more than 10,000 people, and saved more than 20 tonnes of food from going to waste.

Adam's leadership is raw and unfettered by a need for consensus and approval – he rightly considers his purpose to be more important than the bureaucracy that tries to contain it. He's bold and utterly single-minded. His drive and determination can present challenges, as authorities struggle to manage and address his unorthodox 'can-do, will-do' attitude, but so far, he and his team have overcome tough barriers and are experiencing global expansion at a rate most conventional companies would love to emulate.

When asked what captured the imagination of the

thousands of people who are now involved with his project, his reply, in common with many scavenger leaders, is: 'There's nothing complex about it.' It's a straightforward proposition that people can quickly connect to, and Adam provides a compelling, accessible way to deliver on that.

It's bizarre to think that on paper, Adam probably wouldn't qualify for his own job. In fact, if he were to apply for it within a conventional organisation, there's a good chance he wouldn't be interviewed. His considerable talent and leadership skills would be hidden from view. Similarly, there are many who work with Adam who also would have failed the CV test. People who, lacking the conventional career paths or qualifications, nevertheless have risen to play a vital and impressive role in the Project's extraordinary growth.

Adam's light-touch scavenger leadership has successfully brought together and inspired an eclectic group of people from a myriad of backgrounds and experience to pursue the same goal. Adam has only one rule for his team, and he insists that this is all the 'control' that's needed to bring out the best in the people who work for him.

It is pinned up on the wall in his office, and manages to provide the guiding light necessary to steer this phenomenal organisation forward: 'Be Kind.'

5 The key qualities and resources of a scavenger leader

A s we've seen, despite the many differences in scavenger leaders – where they work, what they do, the size of their organisations – they share the powerful scavenger mindset. The reason for their success lies in their ability to think differently, and tap into what truly motivates people.

Abraham Maslow and Douglas McGregor both offer research and thinking that underpins this approach, as does the emerging and increasingly influential science of happiness and positive psychology extolled by Harvard, now an accepted theory worldwide. This is not airy-fairy stuff: it's at the core of what matters most in leading a successful life, as well as successfully leading others. It offers a connection point that's relevant to all of us at any stage in our lives. Maslow's (1943) hierarchy of needs demonstrates how important it is to feel valued and have a sense of belonging; while McGregor's (2008) Theory X and Theory Y research into effective leadership illustrates how a leader's view of their team or teams impacts on their collective success.

The only assumption a scavenger leader makes is that people are capable, resourceful and motivated if they're given the right conditions in which to thrive – and their job is to provide that environment.

Three key qualities are found in every scavenger leader:

1. positive pragmatism
2. resourcefulness
3. ability to innovate.

1. Positive pragmatism

We know that we don't know, but we do know mistakes will happen

What do you know, and what do you need to learn? If you can accept that there are things you can't accurately predict or control, then the process of learning has to be front of mind.

Being pragmatic and facing problems when they arise, builds strong relationships that stand the test of time. As we've seen, from Adam Smith's 5,000 starter emails and Pamela Warhurst's hundreds of conversations to Sophia Parker's questions, scavenger leaders always start with a positive, pragmatic attitude. Bob Chapman simply asked people how they were feeling, which allowed for open-minded questioning and a culture that created success through understanding.

This kind of broad-stroke narrative creates space for people to make decisions, safe in the knowledge that when something unexpected has occurred or hasn't worked out, it would be deemed important information rather than a reason to apportion blame. As we've seen, for Adam Smith this was exemplified by the one rule he gave his team; while in Louise Goulden's case, it was recognising that 'good enough' was the only way to make meaningful progress. When problems arose, the trust and respect which had been built up allowed these leaders to address issues head-on – and move on.

Facing the music

Jazz musician Miles Davis was a brilliant example of a pragmatic leader, once saying: 'If you're not making mistakes, that *is* the mistake.'

He played with his back to the audience, knowing that what mattered most was his ability to communicate and connect with his band, to focus where he had greatest impact, despite any audience disappointment. Herbie Hancock recalls the complete faith Davis showed in his fellow musicians, giving only light-touch instructions to improve their performance, once telling Herbie to just 'play the butter notes'.

He led by example, and by having certainty only in his own talent and that of the people who played with him, the rest was a process of discovery.

This is central to the scavenger mindset: squaring

up to what's really happening, engaging and taking iterative steps to find the best way forward.

Scavenger leaders know that they don't know, so the question they ask is: 'What can we do about that – and how can we make this work for us?' Like the positive pragmatists they are, scavenger leaders acknowledge that mistakes and unexpected outcomes happen. The challenge is not to avoid or ignore problems, but to address them.

Scavenger leaders don't waste time on things that don't work, or spend time on things they can't change. At its roots, positive pragmatism is about compassion for others and ourselves. Scavenger leaders forgive themselves when they're too tired to cope or overwhelmed by responsibility, but they always look for ways to improve. They accept their limitations in order to deal with them, and make sure their coping mechanisms don't become bad habits, descending into destructive behaviours.

Scavenger leaders equip teams to face up to problems, conflict and mistakes. They don't waste time on blame or accusation; instead, they focus on what *can* be done.

Scavenger questions

- What happens when things don't go according to plan?
- What language do you use about failure or mistakes?

◆ How do you learn, and what evidence is there
of this?

2. Resourcefulness

What have we got, and what can we do?

As we've seen, Dr Roger Mills believed in people's
capacity to find their own solutions, and saw beyond
the apparent hopelessness of the Modello neighbourhood to help residents transform both their lives,
and those of many others. He took time to work
with people in a highly effective, resourceful way by
meeting them on their own terms, and slowly but
surely building relationships of trust and respect that
changed their views, not only of what they could
achieve, but also what was really possible.

From fighting to football

Kenyan lawyer Fatuma Abdulkadir Adan's resourcefulness led her to start an initiative to promote peace in
the remote, conflict-plagued Marsabit region of Kenya.

Her love of sport was the inspiration behind setting
up the first-ever village football teams, encouraging
young men to put down their guns and play football
instead with the aspiration to shoot to score, not to
kill. She has gone on to set up a remarkable foundation
(the Horn of Africa Development Initiative), and has
become globally recognised for her promotion of
peace in the region.

Communities are full of resourceful people who have this 'can-do, will-do' attitude and don't buy into conventional wisdom. Being resourceful requires a willingness to challenge assumptions and invite divergent perspectives to build a broader understanding of what needs to happen.

A resourceful leader is always asking: 'So, what? What do we know, what can we do, what do we need to find out?' These were exactly the types of questions I asked myself during the high-street project, and they remain key to ask in any project or initiative.

The mind is like a parachute – it only works when it's open. That says everything you need to know about being resourceful.

Scavenger questions

- How resourceful are you able to be?
- What inspires you and your teams?
- What might you be overlooking?

3. Ability to innovate

What can we be, and how else can this work?

Innovation is a natural by-product of pragmatism and resourcefulness. You can't innovate just by coming up with ideas; innovation requires action and the courage to be creative.

Eliminating fear

In *The New Pioneers* (1999), Thomas Petzinger writes that when Georg Bauer took over as CEO of Mercedes-Benz Credit Corp back in the 1990s, he knew that despite the appearance of success, the organisation would need to change to futureproof itself.

Bauer wanted the new organisation to emerge through a process of trial and error, encouraging employees to determine what worked and what no longer worked. He told other bosses to 'let it grow from the bottom up'.

What Bauer understood was that he needed people to think differently and creatively. For this reason, he instigated the rule to have 'no fear'. He understood that fear ran through the DNA of the company because mistakes had to be avoided at all costs. Bauer knew back then that the future would be all about risk-taking, and leaders needed to support people to take risks, make mistakes and learn to innovate.

I discovered for myself that creating a fear-free environment takes time. Even in an organisation like mine, founded from the ground up, it took time to break out of unhelpful habitual thinking, or reaching for an off-the-shelf remedy based on past experience.

This became even more apparent when I worked with a new political movement that involved a group of intelligent, willing and enterprising people. I'd been asked to help them interrogate how to build meaningful community engagement.

During one of the workshops I delivered, they hit a 'eureka' moment when, as a group, they began to consider an answer to this question: 'What could you do if you didn't have any money?' After an initially cautious response, ideas began to form and connections made that enabled them to break through to a whole new level of thinking and excitement.

The ability to innovate is a state of mind that should be encouraged in everyone, not left to those in a particular department or behind a specific desk. Creativity comes from stretching the mind and widening our sources of inspiration. Walt Disney was said to respond to challenging situations with 'Yes, if': yes, this is possible, if we… How powerful those two words can be. To draw out that level of creativity relies on providing an environment where people feel safe.

Richard Heuer, author of *Psychology of Intelligence Analysis* (1999), underlines the importance of a space that allows people the freedom and time to develop ideas: 'New ideas are often disruptive, and pursuing them carries the risk of failure. People are more likely to advance new ideas if they feel secure.'

Creativity can't be produced on command, and dissolves in the face of overwhelm, anxiety and stress. Setting up a creative space is about more than getting people round a table and having a discussion. Heuer (1999) claims that creativity is a vital skill for intelligence analysts. He cites creative thinking as the way to avoid mental ruts and address bias, but notes that it requires a safe place for its fullest expression.

Creative trailblazer Dave Trott, creative director of the ad agency Gold Greenless Trott, believes 'being creative' isn't about being good artistically, but original thinking – something we can all access given the right conditions (Trott 2019). Archimedes beautifully illustrated how the innovative mind works. His 'eureka' moment didn't appear out of nowhere, but as a result of months of contemplation, deliberation and questioning. That moment of clarity came to him after months in the fog: not behind a desk, but in the bath.

I'm not suggesting we need to install baths in the office(!), but to create a metaphorical and/or physical space that allows the mind to wander and make new connections.

Scavenger questions

- What might be possible that hasn't yet occurred to you?
- How often do you feel surprised?
- When did you last do something that scared you?

The scavenger leader's three key resources

Now that you've been introduced to it, I suspect you'll begin to see examples of scavenger mindset everywhere, and perhaps be reminded of the scavenger within you. If so, then this book has achieved what I hoped it would. Whether it's leading a better life or encouraging your children, teams or communities, developing a scavenger mindset will bring out the best in you.

To navigate wicked problems we must nurture curiosity, encourage active engagement and equip ourselves to expect change and master it. In the adult world the scavenger mindset can feel constrained. Now is the time to reconnect with our inner scavengers and give oxygen to their genius.

Since the days of Sir Isaac Newton, we've placed the greatest value on being in control to maintain order. His view of the world as a mechanism has influenced our understanding of how to organise and structure our lives – especially in the western world. The belief that we can understand the whole by focusing on the parts, and that problems can be identified and fixed with the right skill and expertise, has given rise to reliance on experts and segregated work functions.

The Newtonian belief in cause and effect reinforces what psychologists refer to as the 'Law of Effect': 'Do this and you get that.' Despite all evidence to the contrary, as Margaret Wheatley (2006) says, 'we keep engaging in complex planning for a world we keep expecting to be predictable… with assumptions based on 19th-century physics'.

One outcome of this is a dependency on money to influence behaviour and motivation. While money, status and security are important, scavenger leaders show that the more we feel valued, the less reliant we are on more unpredictable, external elements to build our resilience. For people who have very little, money has huge significance and impact, but scavenger leaders manage to motivate people to go the extra mile without the benefit of money, status or security.

The scavenger mindset taps into the core of what matters most to human beings – which despite massive external change, remains consistent. We thrive when we feel valued, connected and have a level of ownership.

In this state, we:

- contribute more
- become self-motivated
- are willing to collaborate
- can deliver results that exceed expectations.

Ironically, in this state we also need less – less stuff, managing or controlling and cajoling. We've become so accustomed to being valued only by achieving or being seen to achieve predetermined outcomes that it takes time to learn how to invest our energies and time more effectively.

Scavenger leaders focus on where they have the greatest influence. Ensuring that people are at their most productive through creating value, connection and ownership leads to the ability to learn and tolerate challenging situations, giving rise to greater creativity and adaptability.

```
┌─────────────────────────────────────┐
│   Innovative, adaptive behaviour     │
│     Everyday scavenger leaders       │
└─────────────────────────────────────┘
```

```
┌─────────────────────────────────────┐
│   Resourceful, switched-on thinking  │
│ Pragmatic: uncertainty, challenge,   │
│              conflict                │
│     Everyday scavenger leaders       │
└─────────────────────────────────────┘
```

```
┌─────────────────────────────────────┐
│     Connection, value, ownership     │
│   The groundwork (what matters most) │
└─────────────────────────────────────┘
```

With little in our lives that we can guarantee or control, our biggest sphere of influence is within ourselves: how we behave and feel, and the relationships we have with others. Investing in ourselves and our relationships has the greatest impact on how effectively we work with and relate to others, as well as our ability to manage change.

Remember when we stepped outside in the UK

to clap for the NHS during the first phase of the pandemic, how it reinstated our sense of belonging and connection with our community? People spoke of how powerful that connection felt, and how much it meant to them to feel it. That level of connectivity is possible to replicate in a more formal setting, and it really is what matters most to people.

Each of the following resources are free of charge, accessible to all and will be the best investment of time you can make.

Feeling valued

I once had a conversation with a housing association resident after a number of thorny issues had made him angry. He had approached me after a group meeting, and I was struck by how much it had meant to me that, despite his level of frustration, his manner was warm and respectful. At the end of our chat, he told my colleague and I what a difference it had made to him to feel properly listened to, even though we weren't able to deliver the outcome he'd hoped for. Not feeling 'fobbed off' was crucially important to how valued he felt.

No matter where you fit in the hierarchy, feeling valued is the catalyst to releasing potential. This isn't to be confused with feeling entitled or having an inflated sense of self-worth; feeling valued opens the heart and mind. It's free to give but easy to take away.

In my high-street project, the value for people in the community wasn't in the discounts offered or even the products available, but the way in which business owners engaged and built relationships. Scavenger leaders spend time getting to know their teams – listening and learning. The rewards of this simple approach are huge, but can't be faked. People know when they're involved in a box-ticking exercise.

Like most things in life, it's not what you say or even how you say it; it's what you do. Actions always speak louder than words.

Leaders need to lead by example, and this is equally the case in demonstrating how you value and look after yourself. Putting on your own oxygen mask first isn't just a practical and vital action; it also gives others permission to do the same. This is a lesson I learned courtesy of my daughter, who told me that she hadn't realised that looking after herself was important because she couldn't remember me putting myself first. It was a salutary lesson I won't forget.

As a leader, you need to show people how taking care of yourself and making sure you're match-fit is as important as caring for others. Valuing people is about boundaries and knowing your limitations, as well as the limitations of others.

Scavenger questions

- How do the people you live or work with feel valued?
- How do you know that?
- What simple ways make you feel most valued?

Creating connection

Just because you sit in the same room, are on the same Zoom call or live in the same house doesn't guarantee a meaningful connection. In each of the scavenger stories, the connection was first made by people being drawn to the aim or purpose of a project, enhanced by a feeling of community.

Interface introduced a strong connection through its sustainability initiative that allowed people to contribute on a new level. Scavenger leaders invite diverse perspectives, encourage people who don't normally get invited to the table and bring different disciplines together to find a point of connection. With that connection established, you have the foundations of team spirit.

We often take a level of connection for granted. We assume connections exist between people because they work together in a certain department, or share a particular purpose – but there's always more going on below the surface. It's possible to create connection in the most disparate of groups.

Find the connection

However disparate groups may seem, there will be a point of connection if time is taken to locate it.

Consider if Brexit had been an opportunity to explore how people feel valued, connected and have ownership, maybe we would have discovered that we share more than divides us, and found more innovative solutions to the challenges people face.

117

Start with what we can agree on and build from there is both a more powerful and productive strategy.

Connecting to a common purpose, as well as to each other, strengthens any community and creates invisible motivation.

Scavenger questions

- How connected are people to each other, goals and challenges?
- What could you do to enhance a connection?
- What new connections might make a difference?

Creating a sense of ownership

Building ownership is vital to achieve longstanding, confident capacity within an organisation or community.

Showing trust in people to do their jobs is crucial, as is encouraging people to feel: 'It's my job, so let me find a way.' Creating a sense of ownership builds resilience, grows connectivity and reinforces people's feeling of being valued, allowing them to make decisions based on their skills, initiative and experience. Charlene Pedrolie of Rowe Furniture said that the impact of giving ownership to her staff bred a culture of innovation in every corner of the business.

Just before the pandemic, I was asked to run a series of workshops for a pharmaceutical company at a conference they had organised to celebrate the launch of their new purpose. When I arrived, there was a palpable sense of pride in the air. Balloons and T-shirts emblazoned with the new purpose drove home the message in no uncertain terms.

Everyone seemed engaged and on board, but when I asked the workshop participants what this new purpose would mean to them, and how it might make a difference to the way they worked, their response was interesting. They said that this wasn't something they'd even considered, let alone been invited to reflect on. In fact, to some it had seemed a strange question to ask.

But once we began digging deeper into what this purpose might mean for them and how they could bring it to life, the process of taking ownership of the purpose began. Ideas began to spark, and interesting debates and conversations followed.

By the time the workshops finished, it felt like the purpose had found its meaning in the roots of the company, with participants wanting to infuse it into their work. By involving people in the process, they were able to take ownership and felt a stronger connection, sense of value and belonging within the company as a result.

This isn't the exception to the rule: it has been repeated in most of the organisations in which I've worked. Overlooking this kind of engagement makes hard work of motivation while devaluing people's insight, intelligence and ideas, and misses the opportunity to bring people with you. It costs so little to make such a big difference, that ignoring it becomes a reckless oversight.

In Chapter 6 I'll look at how to embed a sense of ownership into the working environment.

Scavenger questions

- What level of ownership exists in your organisation?
- What space is given for people to take ownership?
- What might be preventing letting people take ownership?

Look after the elephant and the rest will follow

If you've created a sense of value, connection and ownership, you've basically done the heavy lifting in terms of motivation. I think of it as the difference between pulling a 10-tonne truck up a hill with your teeth, or jumping in your car and driving up the hill.

Paying attention to these three resources costs nothing but time and a mindset shift. In his book, *The Upside Down of Irrationality* (2011), author Dan Ariely showed that unless someone's role is purely manual, money alone is not a long-term motivator. It's essential, of course: however, the carrot-and-stick approach may appear successful in driving short-term behaviours, but relies too heavily on a source of motivation that is depleted over time.

In their book *Switch* (2010), Dan and Chip Heath show evidence of how self-control and willpower are finite resources that, once used up, aren't easily replenished. Anyone who has ever tried to give up a bad habit or start a good one will know it's not as simple as knowing something isn't good for you, or that you 'should' do something. *Having* to do something is rarely a successful motivator, and 'should' most definitely is not.

Our emotions are what really move us, and are behind most of the decisions we make.

The high-street project was all about creating an emotional connection between the businesses and the community. Rationally, the businesses had little to offer, but emotionally they could beat any of their sophisticated competition. In addition to our brain, we have a mass of neurons in our gut and heart. Even without scientific evidence, we can recognise the power of these two other 'brains' to drive us and influence our thinking. Consider the number of times you hear people saying: 'It just doesn't feel right', 'I have a gut feeling' or 'I haven't the heart to...'

Research has shown that how we feel has a stronger impact on our behaviour than rational thinking: this alone gives us the first step in understanding how we can access our full potential, and galvanise people to achieve far more with less.

There is a growing body of research showing the

significant impact of our emotions on our happiness and success. A Harvard study lasting more than 75 years and involving 724 people from the poorest Boston neighbourhoods and Harvard graduates, discovered that key to physical and psychological wellbeing is quality relationships. (Massachusetts General Hospital and Harvard Medical School 2015)

In his paper 'Altruism, happiness and health', Stephen Post (2005) discovered that:

> The vast majority of people in the European Union and the United States have more material wealth than did their parents; the percentage of these populations that is happy, however, has not increased, and depression and anxiety rates have risen dramatically (Easterbrook, 2004).

Frederickson (2003) summarises two decades of investigation, concluding that positive emotions are linked to a 'broader thought repertoire', or 'big-picture' creative thinking was enhanced. Positive psychology is seen as fundamental to achieving happiness and success, with trailblazing research from Martin Seligman (2002) and the *New York Times* bestseller, *Positive Intelligence* (2012) by Shirzad Chamine.

Why transaction doesn't work to motivate

In his book *The Happiness Hypothesis*, psychologist Jonathan Haidt uses the metaphor of the elephant, the rider and the path to describe the process of motivation.

The rider sitting on top of the elephant represents our rational brain, and to all intents and purposes it appears to be in charge; while the emotional side of our brain is represented by the elephant and represents the real weight in decision making. The path they walk along is the environment in which change takes place.

In our rational world, we use money to motivate and encourage loyalty, we convince people to work towards goals and targets; but for many, this is purely transactional. The mind may be engaged, but the heart isn't – the elephant isn't convinced.

We know that what motivates us to be at our best and how we make decisions is rarely rational. We must engage people's elephants to properly connect with and understand what matters most to them, what inspires their best performance. In doing this, we create a two-way engagement that mobilises a greater sense of ownership.

The beauty of all this is that when we consider what we need, it's basic, available and free. The pandemic has shone a light on this for many of us. What we missed in lockdown wasn't the designer handbag or the flashy car; it was the feeling of connection with other people and the importance of belonging.

In a wicked world where less is known about much more, we need to look after the elephant to cope with fast-changing challenges and uncertainty.

Scavenger questions

- What are you missing out on by not engaging with different perspectives?
- What is stopping you from making this aim?
- How might this be affecting your view of work, and understanding of challenges and opportunities?

Scavenger pioneer #4

Sophia Parker, Little Village

'We already have what we need – we just need to redistribute it.'

Inspirational Little Village founder, Sophia Parker, has witnessed first-hand the truth that we already have what we need – we just need to release it. Or in this case, redistribute it.

Little Village is like a food bank but for clothes, toys and equipment for babies and children up to the age of five. I'd been drawn to Sophia's story as a brilliant example of a scavenger pioneer: someone who, with a clear purpose, had taken small steps to grow her idea into a workable model, mobilising others to help achieve an impact far beyond her initial expectations.

I first met Sophia at the Little Village HQ, in a church hall in Balham, South London. I watched as her colleagues sifted through a vast mound of clothes and baby paraphernalia. Nothing had quite prepared me for the sheer scale of her operation. The number of contributions being made and distributed spoke of the need she had tapped into, and the desire of many families to respond.

The high-ceilinged room had floor-to-ceiling shelves, each shelf housing a line of boxes organised into age groups and filled to the brim with a neatly folded rainbow of clothes, clean and ready for distribution. The volunteers worked on a long, wooden refectory-style table surrounded by a line-up of

125

prams and pushchairs primed and ready for action. There were baby baths, toys, blankets, Moses baskets, cribs and gift boxes filled with vital basics, beautifully presented and chosen with care, transforming the church hall into a dynamic hub for fighting family poverty and inequality.

I was stunned. The room was testimony to the fact that not only is there a clear and desperate need for this transaction between families, but an overwhelming willingness to respond to that need. Little Village reveals the power of a community to take care of each other, if given the right support and conditions to do so, and in a way that no government or local authority would have the power or connection to deliver.

In common with many grassroots initiatives, Little Village was Sophia's personal reaction to an everyday problem. Her desire to put her daughter's old clothes and baby stuff to good use began with reaching out and asking some simple but vital questions to the community to establish need, opportunity and explore logistics.

Her questions quickly revealed the same desire in many other families, while simultaneously exposing the scale of the need for hundreds of desperate families.

Since its launch in 2016, Little Village has helped 2,484 families, 2,474 children and worked with more than 196 volunteers. It has accepted more than £1.3m worth of gifts, and recently launched two new sites in London. From the beginning, Sophia has wanted Little Village to honour families on both sides of the transaction, insisting that any item of clothing, toy or piece of equipment must be clean and ready to use. This is not a dumping ground for chewed-up, broken or dirty baby leftovers.

The tone and culture of the organisation are set by its strapline: 'A gift to your family from ours', making this less about handouts, and more about an open transaction of kindness.

There's a clear recognition of the deep and natural bond that exists between parents and carers, all of whom want the best for their children. Often, it is only a lack of funds or access to support that derails people's hope.

Access to the Little Village service is purposely made as easy and stress-free as possible. Little Village accepts referrals from professional and voluntary organisations working with families in an official capacity, such as midwives, health visitors, food banks and local mutual support groups. Once referred, there is a simple form to fill in but once through the doors, there are no more forms or front-of-desk staff to negotiate. All who enter are respected and given a warm reception. The staff are trained to be supportive, open and friendly, so Little Village has become a place where adults and children feel safe and welcomed. No one is made to feel 'less-than', and the pervading sense is one of 'We're all united in parenthood here'. There is little distinction between those who receive help and those who give it, and the environment is so nurturing that many who come for help go on to become volunteers themselves.

Sophia recognises that wider needs are now being met by Little Village: to feel valued, connected and belong. Making a tangible difference has had a huge, positive impact on everyone who works there, and they also enjoy the circular support network that has grown up around this amazing organisation.

As all our scavenger pioneers have shown, simple kindness and a connecting purpose can produce highly effective and sustainable grassroots organisations. Little Village has created the conditions to bring out the very best in human nature, along with a space where exhausted, fragile, vulnerable people can find sanctuary and acceptance.

Sophia has shown how starting small and fulfilling a specific need can create community relationships that support, inspire and achieve real change from the ground up.

6 How to adopt the scavenger mindset

What I hope you'll recognise from this book is that everything you need to succeed is already within reach. As we've seen, whatever the make-up of your teams, staff or work situation, if you look again and a little deeper, you'll find a set of resources that you may have overlooked. Adopting the scavenger mindset will help you find the talent and answers that lie within.

Over the years, how many initiatives have you adopted, bought into or hired a consultant to introduce, and how many have been as transformational as they promised to be? The scavenger mindset is a one-size-fits-all approach that's shaped by the individuals involved, reveals skills and builds confidence as it grows. With small, significant steps it's possible to unlock potential and ensure sustainable growth, and save considerable time and money.

Adopting a mindset isn't just a case of implementing a model or new framework; it's about changing your own mind about what's possible and important. Like most things in life, the best way to achieve it is to experience it and discover how you can implement it based on your own experience, circumstances and understanding.

However, there are some key areas that allow you to discover the full range of your potential and create the best environment to bring people together. Here are the first three steps to adopting the scavenger mindset:

1. Do the groundwork.
2. Grow transformational communities.
3. Focus on the Here and Now.

1. Do the groundwork

If you haven't done your groundwork, you can't grow anything sustainably. Any gardener will tell you that the single most important factor in successful gardening isn't the quality of seeds, the time you spend in the garden or the expert or tools you buy in – it's the compost. Get this right and everything will grow stronger, be more resilient and reach its full-flowering potential.

As living organisms, humans are just the same. If groundwork is properly prepared, the results will be significantly improved. Your job as a scavenger leader is to feed the soil and create the perfect environment for growth to occur. It's the area where you have the most power, and by getting the groundwork right you'll be giving yourself and others the best chance of success.

It all starts with you:

- How are you?
- How much of your work are you enjoying?
- How much time do you have to make sure you're fit and ready to maintain and improve your role as a leader?
- How do you challenge yourself?
- What inspires you?
- Are there areas you need more help with, or things you'd like to change?

One of the greatest challenges for any leader is to maintain momentum and motivation while avoiding burnout. Leaders often carry the weight of responsibility, stress, anxiety and overwhelm. Are you taking on too much, or clinging on to a need for control? The foundation of your work lies in your ability to face challenges with a degree of emotional balance, and recognise where you need support.

There was no way I was going to be able to write this book without someone to support me. I hadn't written a book before and wanted to make sure it could be the best possible, so I knew I had to find someone to keep me going. Common sense dictates that if you face your fears and recognise your limitations, you can find a way to work through them; they don't need to stop you. I could have found reasons all too easily not to do this, or to give up or lose faith. Find a coach, mentor or someone you can talk to openly and safely, who can inspire your thinking and support your decision making and aspirations.

As we've seen already: put on your own oxygen mask first.

'Audrey Hepburn syndrome'

My nephew and his friend recently visited and, while we were chatting, the TV was on in the background, showing a programme about Audrey Hepburn's life. Flickering on the screen were the familiar images of her in her various glamorous movie roles.

While providing a nice enough backdrop, the programme went largely ignored by us until the images began to change from Hollywood to the footage of her tireless work in developing countries as a UNICEF ambassador. My nephew sat up and took notice, and we turned up the volume to find out more about the incredible difference she had made to so many people.

He was struck by this, admitting he'd only ever thought of her as a pretty actress. It showed how we take people at face value all the time. We assume we know someone and what they're capable of, but there's always more to know about someone – and huge value in finding out what more they can do.

You have a highly talented team of people around you – your role is to let them fly.

You need everyone you work with to be performing at their best and ready to go the extra mile, so it's vital to invest time in getting to know what lies beneath their surface:

- How well are your teams working, both individually and collectively?
- How motivated and well-equipped are they to succeed in uncertain times?

Check in with the people you work with to help identify where support is needed, inspiration is required and hidden potential lies. Building relationships is the single most powerful way to ensure they're able to rise to challenges, persevere when times get tough and develop switched-on thinking to find creative solutions.

If you commit to understanding the needs, fears and motivations of your people, it develops trust and generates insights that benefit everyone. Scavenger leaders do this instinctively, allowing them to achieve their goals without the need for high salaries and big bonuses.

Beyond their name and occupation:

- How much do you know about what matters most to your colleagues and what they're truly capable of?
- What's having the greatest impact on their lives and work?

+ What do you really know about the individuals with whom you work?

Write a list of all the people with whom you work most closely.

+ Who would you never include on that list, and why?
+ Write down what you think you know about them: their qualities, strengths and weaknesses.
+ Why do you think this?
+ What do you think matters most to them?
+ What do you think works in your team?
+ What do you think needs improving?
+ What evidence do you have of this?

We often form our assumptions of what people are capable of based on their CV. But what looks like effectiveness on paper might not translate to their day-to-day work, or how well they work with others. Why might this be? It could come down to stress and anxiety, depression or even neurodiversity. The value in doing this deep dive is that it saves time and money in the long run, and helps you focus on what matters most – as well as where you can have the greatest influence.

The discovery process we went through during the high-street project revealed underlying issues which, if left unchecked, could have resulted in wasted time and money. We designed and facilitated one-to-one and group conversations to gauge what was going on underneath the surface. Working with one of London's largest councils, this process revealed a high level of disconnect between boardroom expectations and staff experience. But it also uncovered a range of opportunities and ideas that repaired the disconnect.

Everyone likes to be listened to and speak openly about what matters. It's important to note that this process is not about day-to-day details; it's about the big picture, the key themes and patterns. Feedback is vital in making this process meaningful:

- What are the key results?
- How does that information get used?
- What was the point of the exercise?

The aim is to discover people's hidden skills, talents and motivations as well as their fears and stresses, so as to identify areas of support and build strong working relationships.

Themes for guided conversations

These conversations require a neutral facilitator, are best facilitated outside of the office and within a one-hour time limit.

Here are some suggested themes and questions to ask.

Connectivity

- Who do you get on with in your team or company?
- With whom do you work best?
- From whom have you learned the most?
- How much interaction is there between departments?
- Can you describe what you have in common?
- How is the company purpose reflected in how you work?
- How much do you know about what other departments do?

During the high-street project, it was only by understanding the fragility of the connection between the businesses that changed our view of what mattered most – which was the need to strengthen that connection. We then focused on bringing businesses together to discuss the point of connection, and the need for a collective approach to make the necessary impact.

Team-building starts with emotion

For England football manager Gareth Southgate, turning his young squad into a team capable of getting to the Euros finals was all about creating an emotional connection between the players. When they first started training together, they had little knowledge of, or commitment to, each other.

Similarly, a large retailer I worked with had many departments operating as silos, with only the occasional crossover or interaction between them. Although everyone was working towards the same outcome, the divisions between the departments reflected the way in which the footballers put their clubs before the national team.

It's all about finding a point on which people can agree. Different departments may have very different ways of working, even different cultures — but wherever there is a crossover, finding that point of connection will be important.

Motivation

- What do you most enjoy about your work?
- How is this reflected in what you do?
- Is there anything you're interested in with which you aren't currently involved?
- What do you fear most in your work?
- How do you address this?
- If you knew you couldn't fail, what would you do at work?
- What keeps you awake at night?
- If there was one thing you could change, what would it be?

As I've suggested in earlier chapters, motivation is rarely just about the paycheck. In my experience, giving people the chance to talk about what matters most to them reveals small but important motivations. These have included the motivation to get home on time to see family, making time for exercise or even volunteering. This type of discovery leads to easy fixes that make a big difference.

Often fear is a key motivator, with negative consequences. In a recent conversation with one executive I was told that she had not taken time out of work for health reasons, as she had been advised, because she hadn't felt able to ask. When working for a large corporation intent on fulfilling their aspiration for innovation, I discovered that undermining their ambition was fear of failure.

1. What's really driving the people you work with?
2. What might you be missing?
3. Would meeting people halfway introduce a greater sense of belonging within the workplace?

Ownership

- What level of ownership do you feel you have at work?
- What aren't you saying that could make a difference?
- How would you like to contribute ideally?
- Where would you like to have more input, and how?
- Who do you think is overlooked, and why?
- Where, how and when do you do your best work?
- What aren't you contributing that you would like to, and why?

As we've seen, understanding where they had ownership was a turning point for the businesses in my local high street. They saw that they had agency when it came to engaging with the community and bringing about change.

It's clear in every scavenger pioneer story that when people feel they're able to make a difference and contribute meaningfully, they invest their time willingly. In much the same way, it was a revelation to staff at a housing association struggling after a takeover that their managers were interested in their thoughts, feelings and opinions.

This is just the first step in really getting to know the people you work with on a more meaningful level. It might point to some new ways to meet some easy-to-fix needs, address work–life balance or reveal a need to address disputes and conflict. It can be the beginning of a more meaningful dialogue, but most importantly you'll be bringing people together to kick-start some switched-on thinking.

Now you have put your focus on relationships rather than roles, what questions has it raised in your mind? What possibilities has it suggested?

2. Grow transformational communities

I define a transformational community as one where:

- learning is at its core
- different perspectives are heard
- a creative environment is nurtured.

Any one of the scavenger pioneers demonstrates that this is not only achievable but desirable, no matter how small you start or how few resources you may have.

Even as a solo entrepreneur you can build a community around you to support and stretch your thinking. I have a small, handpicked group that includes friends and work contacts who have acted as my flexible team of advisers, supporters and inspirers. In the past few years I've also invested in learning, seeking out new sources of inspiration, both online and off, from the arts, lectures, TV and radio programmes and podcasts, and by joining associations and new networks.

In a small organisation, work with the team you have, and/or invite people you know or have worked closely with to become part of your transformational community. As you'll have seen throughout this book, people respond positively in the right environment and under the right conditions. As mentioned previously, for any community to learn, grow and enable transformation, there needs to be a safe space in which to operate openly and creatively. Amy Edmondson (1999) describes this type of safety as 'the shared belief that the team is safe for interpersonal risk-taking'. As an individual, you need to feel able to take on feedback and accept where you may need support or guidance. You need to be unafraid to speak up. The role of facilitator is also important in promoting trust and respect and creating a productive environment. This needs patience, perseverance and a clear eye on the end goal and the point of connection. A transformational community isn't about building a framework to drive consensus; it's almost the exact opposite. It needs not only to tolerate differences of opinion but welcome them.

Bringing diverse voices together requires careful curation, but can have an instant impact.

Trying something different works

Dave Trott (2019) quotes the example of how having different perspectives around a table saved the day for AMV BBDO, an advertising agency tasked with a Sainsbury's brief that required an increase in customer spend of £3bn over two years.

As all the brand executives scratched their heads and grew anxious about their task, a young planner proffered the business perspective rather than a brand perspective: observing that in terms of the number of weekly customers, they only had to raise each customer's spend by £1.50 a visit to meet their target, so transforming a huge task into something within easy reach.

The 'Try Something Different Today' campaign was born – which not only reached their target, but surpassed it.

Not everyone will feel confident about speaking up, and some will want to dominate. In a community like this, everyone needs the chance to speak. In her book *Time to Think* (1999), Nancy Kline suggests giving people up to three minutes of uninterrupted time to speak. This not only means people can think without worrying about someone interrupting or talking over them, but also that people learn to listen. We're so used to being interrupted that we find silence awkward, but to be properly heard and think deeply, we need uninterrupted airtime.

Also, consider ways in which people can contribute both before and after a meeting, so as to capture emerging thoughts and ideas, and give them options for having their voice heard. Even if you feel that everyone knows each other, make sure you check in with them and give time for introductions. Think of a way that makes introductions easy and meaningful, but not onerous, as this is an important part of seeing beyond titles or roles to help build relationships.

For example, outdoor clothing retailer Patagonia has a rule it calls 'MBA' (Management By Absence): even if managers are present in meetings, giving space for others to talk and make suggestions has produced powerful results.

Learn how to be OK with disagreements and challenges: see this as an intention to improve, and an indication that someone is fully engaged with the process. Take a leaf out of Walt Disney's book and allow emphasis to be on how to improve. Ask for suggestions about what isn't working, how it can be improved on, how might the process work better and who can contribute to that discussion.

It's also important to allow people to express frustration, even anger. Be aware of understanding gaps, barriers and assumptions: a good facilitator flags up when assumptions are being made, or jargon is used that might not be familiar to everyone. I've been in many meetings where the language wasn't familiar to me, and mentioned earlier in Chapter 1 what a huge disconnect this proved to be when trying to create an initiative designed for community engagement. Language has huge impact, and requires careful consideration.

Once the high-street project was up and running, I made a point of setting up meetings with other key stakeholders, from local organisations to the local authority, keeping them involved and up-to-date with what was happening. This helped enormously in the long run, when we needed their support or they wanted to contribute.

In larger organisations, find a way to share findings and involve others. Companies often use 'town hall' meetings to get people involved by sending in questions: those that gain the most votes have to be answered by senior executives. A scavenger leader asks for suggestions on how best to answer a question or improve a process.

Bob Chapman writes that, to encourage the widest possible involvement, it's important to have good guidelines, but not many rules: 'Just enough structure means we have established some guardrails but not imposed so many rules that they stifle individuality, personal judgement, innovation or creativity' (Chapman and Sisodia 2015).

You might wish to adopt a one-liner, like Bauer's 'no fear' or Adam Smith's 'Don't be a Dick' (more recently upgraded to 'Be Kind'). For you, what one line would say all that's required to keep people operating productively and openly? As a company, Patagonia has a 'no meetings at lunchtime' rule because it hopes people will be outdoors or exercising.

Group guidelines are a useful starting

point for a transformational community:

- ◆ What will people expect from themselves and each other?
- ◆ What do people want to learn about?
- ◆ How will you celebrate?
- ◆ How will you share?
- ◆ What do you do when something goes wrong?
- ◆ What's your biggest challenge?

An important part of growing a transformational community is to understand that small actions are the most powerful way to learn, and are the prerequisite for innovation. Remember the lessons from scavenger leaders – big is not better. As we've seen, smaller actions are more likely to be achieved, less onerous to learn from and produce more immediate results. We learn more from mistakes, unexpected outcomes and having a go than theorising or just repeating what has gone before. It's always worth remembering the simple human truths that bind us: no matter what the experience, status or profile, underneath we all have the same needs and insecurities. No one wants to look foolish, feel irrelevant or that they don't belong.

We need to consider how to take the fear out of learning. Being right is not the answer. It may sound weird, but in complex times where there are no neat answers, what would being 'right' mean? When people act from a place of fear it can translate into aggression, defensiveness and sometimes rudeness. Giving people space to have their reaction and let it dissipate allows them to regroup, simmer down and come back ready to discuss.

When things get heated, don't join in the drama; instead, find time to discover what matters most to each party and that all-important point of connection. But be clear about boundaries: if someone is being disruptive in a non–creative way, it needs to be dealt with – and give people the benefit of the doubt whenever possible.

Most of us are trying to be decent humans; if someone isn't, that should be dealt with away from the glare of others. Whatever the framework, build in, review and reframe sessions on a regular basis.

3. Focus on the Here and Now

As Sir Arthur Conan Doyle (2011[1927]) wrote in *The Case-Book of Sherlock Holmes*, 'When you have eliminated all which is possible, then whatever remains, however improbable, must be the truth'.

This is about getting clarity on what you have in the here and now. Appraise your situation for what it is, not what you think it should be or expect it to become. What can you be sure of; what's within your control? Look at the positives and the areas in which you have influence. Then consider what might not be in your control, what you're relying on happening but might not turn out according to plan. What might be the result of that? What you're left with is what's possible, which requires an ability to think beyond normal boundaries.

Focusing on the here and now, in relation to your goal or purpose, will help raise important questions, and encourage new thinking.

The economist John Maynard Keynes recognised that: 'The difficulty lies not so much in developing new ideas as in escaping from the old ones' (quoted in Drexler and Minsky 1987). This process of looking at the here and now helps everyone to focus on the present without being hijacked by a 'this is how we do it' mindset.

Exercise: the Here and Now

(My high street example)

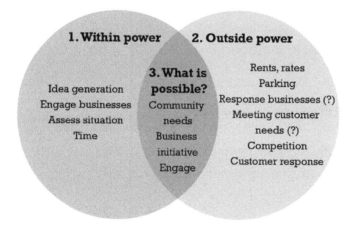

This diagram shows how I first scoped out the high-street project. The middle section (3) represents

147

the ideas that emerged after I'd brought businesses together to reimagine what might be possible.

This exercise works on a number of levels, but most importantly will help you establish how tame or wicked your challenges may be. Understanding the nature of a problem or opportunity helps guide you to the right approach, and who can and should be involved.

Here are some questions to ask yourself in each section.

1. What's within your power?

- What is certain here?
- How do you know this to be true?

Work through what's within your power when it comes to people, resources, ideas, targets, partnerships, systems and processes.

- What's working well?
- What needs improvement?
- What conversations need to take place?
- What do you need to find out?
- What are limitations, restraints?
- What might go wrong?
- What do we need to safeguard against?
- What is the feedback/decision process?
- What actions can be agreed on?

This will give you a view of the priorities, enable

you to establish key actions and help identify gaps that you have the power to fill.

2. What's not within your power?

- What situations are out of your control? Might this change?
- How do you know this to be true?
- How can you address this? Do you need to?
- What options are there that you might not have considered?
- Who might be important to talk to?
- What might go wrong?

3. What *might* be possible?

What else can you do? As we've seen, one of the strongest characteristics of scavenger leaders is that they're not afraid to ask big, seemingly impossible questions.

A big-picture question can bring people together and encourage switched-on thinking. The process of identifying the question can be as informative as the reaction you get from asking it, and it often arises from a deep dive-facilitated conversation.

When you begin to ask impossible questions, you start to realise that they're only impossible to answer because of the framework within which you've been accustomed to thinking.

Here are some examples of 'impossible' questions

that provided the catalyst for transformational actions:

- The high-street project – how can we improve the high street with no money, resources, experience or permission?
- The small charity – how can we get the help we need without having a budget to pay for it?
- The retailer – what is a customer in today's world, and how can we best serve them?
- The local authority – without extra funding, what can our role be in supporting healthier communities?
- The leadership guru (Hamel 2009) – instead of engineering our operating model for efficiency, how could we go about re-engineering our management model for innovation?

Scavenger innovation

If being right is no longer the answer, what's the right question to be asking?

Questions like these knock down the walls of conventional thinking. The businesses that set 'impossible' questions have an approach that's similar to the world-class scientists and engineers who have transformed what we believe to be possible in the world. There's a saying in the coaching world that no dream is impossible if it's humanly possible and you believe it to be so – and this is reflected in the scavenger mindset. There are no right or wrong answers, but asking seemingly impossible questions is the beginning of a learning process that takes you beyond the realms of established thinking. A skilled facilitator can help people to step out of their comfort zone into the realm of impossible possibility.

Adopting the scavenger mindset is first and foremost about looking again and deeper at what's already available to you, and recognising the true value of that which already exists. First, do your groundwork to build powerful productive relationships. Second, grow a transformational, learning-focused community around complex challenges. Create an environment that allows for high-level contributions from everyone, focused on clear aims or ambitios. Third, focus on the Here and Now, where it's possible to ask 'impossible' questions.

This is a mindset that's fit for 21st-century complexity. It works from the inside out, building strong foundations that can support people to form communities and organisations that can face the challenges of uncertainty, steering them on their way to achieving far more than they ever thought possible.

7 Downhill to a brighter future

I've now realised that the scavenger mindset is my default setting. It has kept me going through tough times, and continually stretches my thinking and learning. It has helped me to persevere with an open mind, allowing me to find small pleasures in where I am, while moving towards a brighter future. This has built stamina, which in the past two years has proved invaluable, and enabled me to write this book at a time when I've been spinning a great number of plates.

In common with most people, 2020 marked the beginning of a challenging year. Even before Covid-19 arrived, my landscape was looking fairly arid. The previous year my daughter had been diagnosed with an illness that needed my support and focus, so I began 2020 already feeling depleted, but in February she finally got the supported she needed so I turned my attention back to a growing to-do list that included selling our home. Our new home, which we moved into later that year, required considerable renovation, the main body of which was due to take between three and four months; suffice to say it didn't, and at the time of writing, 14 months on, builders are still on site, with costs escalating, along with levels of anxiety. Then, after a tough year, in late 2021 my mum was diagnosed with Alzheimer's.

Throughout this time, my scavenger mindset kept me moving forward, challenging me and keeping me proactive and productive.

In the midst of this whirlwind, I knew I had to focus on the here and now, on what *could* be accomplished, considering what I'd be able to cope with; I knew I needed to find something positive to do. For years, people had told me I should 'do something' within the speaking arena, building further on the presentations and workshops involved in my work. I joined the Professional Speakers' Association and soon after, decided to enter its prestigious national speaking competition.

My scavenger mindset reasoned this would be a great learning opportunity: to find out whether I had what it takes to become a public speaker, discover whether my material would land with an expert audience, and get feedback from some of the best speakers in the world. It took me way out of my comfort zone, but my focus wasn't so much on the result but the value of the experience. My talk was about how to inspire people to look again and look differently at their potential, drawing on the powerful lessons of grassroots leadership.

Not only did I win my heat but I went on to win the competition, being named Emerging Speaker of 2020. My scavenger mindset led me to the discovery that I am a good speaker and my material is of real interest, giving me the confidence to write this book. It was a great example of how challenging yourself really pays off, whatever your age or however established you may be in your career, or how stuck you may feel in your life in general.

After that, I used my competition win to deliver a series of talks aimed at inspiring people to take on challenges that might feel daunting, to let go of perfection and stretch their thinking around what could be possible. Through this my confidence grew, and I decided to take a formal coaching qualification. My belief that we all have the answers within is beautifully echoed in the coaching approach. Having qualified, I was drawn to a new specialist coaching qualification to support people to overcome addictive behaviours and find healthier ways to cope with stress and anxiety. I gained so much from these courses, not least of which was networking with a wide range of extraordinary people who were demonstrating their own scavenger mindsets.

Despite living through a rollercoaster time, the scavenger mindset kept me rooted in what mattered most, allowing me to achieve things that were way beyond my expectations. Along the way, I've realised that learning is a messy business. You need time to step back, reflect and keep going through the 'stuckness', which is just as important as when you're in flow.

My scavenger mindset has helped me navigate turbulent times, and helped me to understand what I really need. In this overwhelming world, it's so easy to feel utterly without traction and buried under the sheer weight of stuff and things. Learning, as I have, that you do have the resources to manage and thrive – no matter what is thrown at you – is life-changing. Whatever you have right now is what you need. I know that.

I'd like to end with a story that demonstrates this in a deeply personal way.

My father was diagnosed with early-onset dementia when he was in his fifties – around the age I am now. There are echoes of him throughout this book – the way he encouraged and challenged me, gave me belief in my own abilities, inspired my resourcefulness and valued that which others might overlook.

As you'll see in Chapter 8, Dad was my first scavenger hero. After he died, my brother and I cleared out the cellar containing all his beloved tools. In one corner there was a filing cabinet filled with his meticulously handwritten accounts, insurance and car paperwork. At the back was a folder labelled 'Retirement'. It was filled with articles and pictures of cottages in the Ardèche in the south of France, where we'd gone on holiday a couple of times.

Unbeknown to us, he'd been planning to sell the

family home and move to this little paradise after his retirement. His notes revealed he'd been imagining a life of self-sufficiency: growing lavender, vegetables, making wine and spending the evenings sitting out in the warmth of the ebbing sun with my mum, going for walks and swimming in the nearby river.

It was a poignant find, and so incredibly sad that he didn't get close to fulfilling this dream. It haunted me for some time, until a few months later when I was talking this through with Mum and she told me about a conversation she'd had with Dad just before his illness took hold.

They had been sitting together on a little sofa, drinking morning coffee, watching the birds and discussing their next garden project. Dad had put his hand in hers and told her that, for all the striving in his life to make the world a better place and the frustrations he'd had in trying to do that, he realised he had what he'd always wanted right here: his wife, his family, his house and our dog.

This was where he had found his power and place of peace. Perhaps if Dad had understood this, felt this before, it may have had a more positive impact on his life experiences.

More than anything else, this taught me that there isn't a perfect time to act. If you keep tweaking, are indecisive, scared or passive, the world will simply swirl past, leaving you for dust. This year hasn't been the perfect backdrop I'd envisaged for writing my book

– there were curveballs appearing at every juncture, and really noisy ones at that. I didn't ever get to have the quiet space at the back of the house to set up an office and overlook my garden, or the headspace to feel calm, relaxed and fully focused. But that's life.

In times of stress and overload, the scavenger mindset is forgiving, so I gave myself time away from the book and the host of naysayers in my head. This gave me a much-needed pause to reflect, rework and reframe. If you pause, even for a few minutes, your body will tell you what you need, and you must listen. That said, without a clear deadline I could've gone on tweaking, fussing and finding endless excuses for not being quite ready to let go of the manuscript. I could've kept waiting for the moment when I could sit back with absolute certainty that I'd written exactly what I wanted, how I wanted. Thankfully, my scavenger mindset relieved me of that burden – knowing it's a dead-end expectation.

Like our primitive ancestors, the hunter-gatherers, who had to keep moving so as not to deplete their resources, the contemporary world requires us to keep moving forward, to keep learning, to keep finding new inspiration.

I hope this book has inspired new thinking, a fresh sense of possibility and a powerful new way of leading in uncertain times. I hope it's also a reminder that, much like my dad discovered, the things that really matter are nearly always within reach – and will bring their own benefits and rewards.

8 My scavenger heroes

Much to my delight, I come across a new scavenger hero almost every day or someone sends me an example, so this list is constantly being updated. I could probably produce a list by sector, but for now, just know that this is far from being definitive: a glimpse into the range of people who have inspired me, and demonstrate excellent scavenger credentials.

Some you may know; some may be new to you. Scavenger leaders are perhaps most successful at finding the kind of fulfilment that transcends a need for others' approval. What all of these heroes demonstrate is that the scavenger mindset is everywhere and in everyone – so here, in alphabetical order, are my latest scavenger heroes.

Jane Addams

This middle-aged, middle-class, white American set up a community space in a deprived neighbourhood in Chicago back in the 1900s. She demonstrates how little humans have changed and how, when our basic needs are met, we're all capable of far more.

Inspired by the settlement houses of Europe, particularly Toynbee Hall in London's East End, Addams set up Hull House

> to provide a centre for higher civic and social life; to institute and maintain educational and philanthropic enterprises and to investigate and improve the conditions in the industrial districts of Chicago. (Addams 1910)

The reason why Addams is one of my scavenger heroes is that she brought together people from completely different cultures, asking: 'How to encourage cooperation with others who differ?', and 'How to stimulate the desire to associate at all?'

This was achieved by focusing on everyday experiences – parenting, shopping, cooking – that everyone could relate to, and by making a virtue of informality. She believed that the

> things which make men alike are finer and better than the things that keep them apart, and that these basic likenesses, if they are properly accentuated, easily transcend the less essential differences of race, language, creed and tradition. (Addams 1910)

Her autobiographical book, *Twenty Years at Hull House* (1910), contains lessons that remain as vital and relevant today as they were more than 100 years ago.

Purnima Devi Barman

This is a remarkable story about how one woman saved a bird from near extinction in her home state of Assam, north-east India. The greater adjutant suffered not only from being an ugly bird, but one that was considered to be vermin and even a bad omen – so much so, that killing these birds was considered to be acceptable.

Barman, a wildlife biologist and conservationist, asked herself the impossible question: 'How can I get people to actually care about this bird?' In the early days she was mocked, even ridiculed, with people asking: 'Why should we care about this bird? Will she pay us to care?' The answer to that was a resounding 'No'. And yet Barman was successful in finding a solution to her impossible question, convincing people not only to save the adjutant, but in doing so, transforming their own lives.

Barman knew that to answer that question she needed to bring people with her, to win their hearts and minds and persuade them to change their views and behaviour. She realised that people weren't hostile because they were bad, but because they had been misinformed or hadn't been taught to value wildlife.

Her first step was to build relationships – so she met people, listened to community concerns and took small actions to earn trust and respect. In particular, she spoke to women who, in her culture, were often overlooked and excluded from decision making. She saw the potential to build a network of support, and convinced the women to take ownership of the birds.

Together, they created initiatives that they could run and take part in, from running 'baby showers' for baby birds to weaving fabric featuring the bird's motif. In this way she built a small army of women who took over the care of the birds, and in turn empowered women, giving them the opportunity to take charge and take ownership, which transformed their lives. Barman was quoted as saying: 'I think the world should know about this huge force of women' (Sohn 2021).

I probably don't need to explain why Barman is one of my scavenger heroes. It's almost poetic that she actually saved a scavenger – a bird that had been dismissed, disliked and overlooked but became the source of such inspiration and transformation.

- Working with what's already available (and frequently overlooked).
- Asking an impossible question.
- Focused on what matters most to people.
- Started small.
- Asked questions, learned, built relationships.
- Valued people, connected with them and gave them ownership.

Francis Crick

Crick is one of the Nobel Prize-winning scientists who played a crucial role in deciphering the structure of the DNA molecule. However, he is one of my heroes not because of this life-changing discovery, but the approach he took to work and the relationships he built within it.

To the uninformed, scientists might be seen as introverted geniuses hidden in basement laboratories, surrounded by textbooks and microscopes. But the truly brilliant scientists are gifted innovators with highly creative and progressive minds. Sydney Brenner, who worked closely with Crick, offered insights into why Crick's approach became so successful. He described how Crick asked important questions. Brenner referred to this as an ability to 'crystallise' key questions, something Crick himself recognised, believing it was finding the right questions to ask that set their work apart and led them to success (Web of Stories 2017).

Equally important was that Crick insisted you should 'never restrain yourself' (Web of Stories 2017), and Brenner recalled there being only one rule in their shared office: that you had to be able to say anything that came into your head, however stupid or wrong it might seem, because of the ideas it might spark. This also included criticising or challenging someone. Crick believed that being able to criticise someone was actually the height of friendship – ensuring you were stretched to your fullest potential and your work rigorously examined.

But what underpinned this highly productive and innovative environment was a feeling of safety.

Jamal Edwards

The announcement of the death of music entrepreneur Jamal Edwards in February 2022 sent shockwaves through the music industry, and shone a light on the life of a young man I hadn't previously heard of, but who was one of the best examples of scavenger leaders I've come across.

Jamal was inspiration personified: through his actions he transformed the lives and hopes of so many people while changing the map of music in the UK forever. Edwards began his extraordinary career at the age of 16, with just a handheld video camera. He set up the YouTube channel SB.TV, and began by filming artists rapping and performing: in this way, he gave creative space for artists to find an online audience. At the time there were very few UK rap artists in the top 100, and US rap dominated the charts.

Edwards's online platform was responsible for kick-starting the careers of some of the biggest artists in the UK, including Stormzy and Ed Sheeran. He may have begun with very little, but by his early twenties he was a millionaire. Despite his money, very little changed.

His love of music and the people who made it continued to be his focus. His ability to build rapport with his artists is what many consider to be the reason for their success. As his success grew, so did the range of work and support he offered. Often under the radar, he supported community initiatives, working out ways in which he could invest in young people. He was also involved in launching initiatives such as the Spirit of London Award.

In his 31 years he achieved more than most of us will do in a longer lifetime. Listening to the many tributes, I was so struck by his kindness and generosity. He was clearly talented, ambitious, innovative and resourceful, and seemed to have had an in-built sense of the power of giving back. Contributing to life was something that mattered so much to him.

In an interview on Radio 1Xtra, he explained that even when he was stacking shelves he was actually investing in his business, saving up money to buy a camera to launch what became a music revolution.

He is the epitome of a scavenger leader – someone who started in small ways with nothing but his own imagination, and a vision to build something significant.

Theaster Gates

When I first came across Theaster Gates he was a world-renowned potter, but had more recently become famous for his work regenerating the South Side of

Chicago, an area he described as full of dilapidated buildings that had been left to rot: somewhere people either leave or get stuck.

As a potter, Gates described how he understood how to shape things, and the process of learning that is required to do so. His cultural connection to the area drove his own ambition to shape the space differently. In 2006, Gates bought a former candy store for $130,000; two years later he bought the place next door for $16,000. The former crack house was transformed into the Black Cinema House, hosting screenings and discussions on African American films. The candy store became the Archive House, housing a micro-library. Through a web of enterprises, Gates invested back in his town, which now includes a studio, the non-profit Rebuild Foundation.

Buying the dilapidated neoclassical building from the city for just $1, he raised money for renovation so that it could become a centre of beauty, inspiration and community. The building is now part-library, community centre and gallery. More than just a renovation, this has brought a sense of belonging and pride to the area.

Gates (2015) calls it 'redemptive architecture', which isn't about gentrification, but creating concrete ways for existing residents to feel that 'culture can thrive where they live, and that there is reason to believe good things will follow'. Gates is a scavenger hero because of his resourcefulness, belief and the way he demonstrates how every community has something of value. His scavenger mindset is summed up by the quote: 'Making great things out of nothing, spending a whole lot of time trying stuff' (Gates 2015).

Dee Hock

As mentioned in Chapter 3, Hock was a phenomenally innovative and powerful leader. His design of the Visa organisation – a self-organising, evolving system that mirrored the principles of evolution and nature – has proved how much more people are capable of when given the conditions to thrive.

Hock was born in Utah, and from an early age showed the signs of a truly original thinker. He walked away from several fast-track jobs, railing against the hierarchical, rule-following approach that he said was 'stifling creativity and initiative from the grassroots' (quoted in Mitchell Waldrop 1996). I couldn't have said it better myself! As far back as the 1970s, Hock described command–and–control structures as 'not only archaic but increasingly irrelevant. They [are] becoming a public menace, antithetical to the human spirit and destructive to the biosphere' (quoted in Mitchell Waldrop 1996).

He knew that Visa couldn't be designed from the top-down because payment systems were different in every country and jurisdiction. Any concern about what would happen to Visa when he left proved unnecessary: when he exited in 1984, Visa never missed a beat. Hock coined the term 'chaordic organisation' (quoted in Mitchell Waldrop 1996) to describe the behaviour of any self-organising, self-governing organisation or system that harmoniously exhibits characteristics of both order and chaos.

From 1992 onwards, Hock spent his time working as a speaker, adviser and writer, encouraging chaordic concepts to emerge, and aiming to introduce more equitably distributed power and wealth and more harmony between humans and biosphere. He is quoted as saying: 'I have no intention of giving a precise organisational plan and telling you how to implement it' (in Mitchell Waldrop 1996). Instead, he asserted that the best approach is to have a 'clear sense of direction and a set of beliefs, and that lies within you. The question is how do you evoke it?'.

Stephen C. Macdonald

The first, the original, the man whose initials form the abbreviation I've been using for scavenger mindset – ScM – is in many ways my initial inspiration for this book.

In common with many scavenger leaders, from the outside he may not have struck anyone as a hero. Granted, my father was a good-looking man, won a scholarship to Cambridge and went on to captain the Scotland hockey team. His career went from the church to being one of the founding members of the World Development Movement (now Global Justice Now), an organisation that worked to end poverty and injustice, and ended in adult education. But he never reached the dizzying heights of six-figure salaries or a position of global influence, which was perhaps what had been expected of him.

As a father he didn't necessarily fit the mould either. As a teenager, I must admit to wishing that he was more like other people's dads: that he'd play golf, hang out at the local pub, be 'normal'. Instead, at weekends, he spent hours working on the house, growing vegetables in the garden, mending the pond (ours and the one in the village), making beer, getting involved politically ('don't complain if you're not prepared to do something about it'), trying to create a wildlife meadow, endlessly painting the many windows in our house or fixing things in his cellar.

This may not sound inspiring, but you weren't in the room with him when he talked about the world and its possibilities. He challenged the status quo, and had a belief in people to be so much more than the external shell from which we judge them. His passion, energy and determination to rid the world of its inequalities and division made me see beyond the edges of my village-based world.

But through him I also learned the nuances, the complexities of life, that there's more to someone than the role they inhabit or are given in life. He once said to me:'Just because I'm your dad and an adult doesn't mean to say I have all the answers, or that I'm right.' His honesty about how he felt wasn't always easy to navigate when I was a child, but it made me realise that however grown up or successful you appear to be, we're defined by how valued we feel (or have felt), how connected we are and what sense we have of our own power.

I remember vividly a time when Dad felt powerless when, despite having evidence collected over years of an impending famine in Africa, it took a scruffy Irish musician to cut through and make the difference with a concert called Live Aid. It was the moment I realised that sometimes being right is not the answer. If you don't bring people with you, don't use the right language or fail to engage people properly, no matter how right you are, how urgently you feel your purpose or goal to be to bring people with you, you must first discover what matters most to them – and what will move and motivate them.

Dad wasn't perfect (thank the Lord – can you imagine having to follow perfect? I'm not sure I would've believed in it anyway). He was sensitive – it was always my dad and I that cried at the end of *The Railway Children*. Like most humans he was a mix of light and shade, but he was stimulating, respectful and challenging. When I once exclaimed that the world wasn't fair, he replied: 'Well, whoever said it would be?' He also encouraged us to keep learning, and not in a purely conventional way. When I got into trouble at school, he didn't assume the school was justified. He would talk to me, and demand that I was involved in any conversations and wasn't left in the corridor while my fate was decided.

When both my sisters married in the same year, he told me to remember that 'marriage is not the only option, and having children is not a prerequisite for happiness'. His saying: 'If a job's really worth doing, it's worth doing, even if it's done badly,' gave me permission to have a go, learn, be curious and not believe in perfection as the goal; rather, to recognise that the magic is the process.

He made the most of what he had by being engaged with life, except perhaps with his own wellbeing. My brother and I have vivid memories of what we now realise was his poor mental health. Like many people of his generation, he'd had his fair share of childhood trauma, which was never properly treated so sat deep within him, occasionally bubbling up and over on to all of us.

He was in his fifties when we discovered that his increasingly strange behaviour was, in fact, early-onset dementia – Pick's Disease, to be precise. Over the next 20 years he slowly, painfully disappeared in front of our eyes until he was little more than the shell he stood up in. There were fewer and fewer sparks of recognition or connection. He limped his way to death, a mockery of the way he had lived, with my amazing, stoic, pragmatic mum looking after him for as long as it was safe to, keeping the worst from us, and allowing us to crack on with our lives as best we could.

Sometimes Dad didn't make life easy for himself or others, but he was the champion of the possible, the advocate for the overlooked, and more than anything he showed me that what really matters in life is to be engaged. The positive impact he was able to have on me was in no small measure because of my mum. She was the tame to his wicked. She provided a calm, safe environment and could hold the space around his emotional roller-coaster, giving him a strong foundation. She also went to university in her forties, qualifying as a social worker and continuing her education into her fifties, when she entered management just at the time Dad's illness hit.

George Mpanga
(aka George the Poet)

Born in north-west London, Mpanga is a spoken word performer, artist, activist, social commentator, award-winning podcaster and, for me, a scavenger leader personified. What makes him a true scavenger hero is how he engages in the world with a passion that sets light to everything he touches. His gentle, warm voice belies a fierce intelligence that transcends conventional boundaries, covering a wide variety of subjects, beautifully reflected in his podcast: *Have You Heard George's Podcast?*

He was nominated in six different categories in the 2020 British Podcast Awards: Best Current Affairs, Moment of the Year, Smartest Podcast, Best Arts and Culture, Best Fiction and Best New Podcast. He won four, along with a special award. There isn't just breadth to Mpanga; there's also profound depth. He coined the term 'nobodyness', describing it as 'a thing that's chasing a lot of us, it's like you're nothing – you're not counted' (Mead 2020).

Mpanga isn't just a powerful speaker; he also puts passion into action, drawing on his life experience and beliefs to great effect within conventional systems. For much of his twenties he has been working with prisoners across the UK. In this way he has gained insights into the minds of incarcerated men, and spoken publicly to promote his discoveries and ideas:

Instead of assuming these guys have nothing to contribute, my lecture is about asking what assumptions we can make that would lay a foundation for them to optimise their time so they will look back, not with shame, but with gratitude and relief. (Thorpe 2021)

In spending time understanding the reality of prison life, he has developed a new approach that could transform the lives of prisoners: 'What matters is being part of a social scene that provides the emotional stability and hope that enables someone to lean into their better nature' (Thorpe 2021).

He asks big questions of society, and offers real hope for prisoners everywhere.

Srinivasa Ramanujan

January 1st, 1913

Dear Sir,

I beg to introduce myself to you as a clerk of the accounts department of the Port Trust Office in Madras on a salary of only about £20 a year. I am now about 23 years of age. I have had no university education, but I have undergone the ordinary school course. After leaving school I have been employing any spare time at my disposal to work at mathematics. I have not trodden through the regular conventional course that is followed in a university course, but I am striking out a new path for myself. I have made a special investigation of divergent series in general and the results I get are termed by the local mathematicians as startling… (in Veisdal 2021)

So begins a letter of introduction from Ramanujan to G.H. Hardy, at that time one of Britain's most distinguished mathematicians and Professor of Mathematics at Trinity College, Cambridge.

In many ways, the letter says it all. Without any

formal training, lacking any of the qualifications or even the language, this young man's genius may well have been lost to the world had it not been for Hardy's curiosity and instinct. Despite enclosing examples of his discoveries and theories, other letters went unanswered or politely declined; the recipients were unconvinced that he could have anything of note to offer. Ramanujan offered incredible results, but no proof of his process.

As Hardy is believed to have said of his results: 'This must be true, because no one would have the imagination to invent them' (Brown 2015). The partnership between the conventional, linear Hardy and the intuitive, imaginative Ramanujan, able to discern patterns in things others couldn't, went on to become one of the most important of all time in the world of mathematics.

For me, not known for my mathematical abilities, it's the impact Ramanujan had on those around him that was so significant and important. Hardy saw the genius, but knew that he would need to mentor Ramanujan in the basics of the mathematical process, if he was to get his work published and accepted in the wider world.

Ramanujan is best known for his work on number theories and infinite series, but for me the magic isn't in his mathematical achievements; rather, in the impact he had on his contemporaries. He blew the doors off their thinking, challenging them to rethink what they believed was possible. He was a disruptive force of nature that left the landscape of mathematics forever changed.

There are many reasons why Ramanujan is a scavenger hero. Clearly he was a genius, as well as resourceful, determined, pragmatic, with an abundance of imagination. But that's not the reason why I see him as a hero. It's the heroism of the partnership that I'm so struck by: a collision of cultures and mindsets woven into a powerful partnership.

Hardy was considered one of the foremost mathematicians of his generation. Operating at the very heart of the British establishment, he was a man whose life revolved round numbers, logic, linear thinking and rationale. In the film *The Man Who Knew Infinity* (2015), it's implied that the effort to 'tame' Ramanujan's thinking to fit with the status quo came at a considerable personal cost. He eventually learned the processes necessary to demonstrate proof, but it drained his spirit and energy. His knowledge and imagination, plucked from the ether, handed him results that would never be accepted until he could demonstrate, line by line, how he had arrived at his conclusions.

To be published and 'taken seriously', Ramanujan had to learn how to communicate a logical process. The partnership didn't just transform the world of mathematics; it also transformed each man. Hardy admitted he had learned as much from his 'student' than his student had learned from him. In the end, Hardy was fundamentally changed by this young, spiritual, brilliant man, and he mourned the early death of his friend profoundly.

As a scavenger, I relate to Ramanujan's impatience in having to explain his thinking in a way that doesn't come naturally. I know that feeling where flights of imagination take you to a place that just sings and makes complete sense to you, but you lost the map of how you got there along the way, if indeed it ever existed.

It's not enough to know; you have to show. In a similar way, it has been a struggle for me to articulate the processes necessary to adopt the scavenger mindset, and explain why it's so powerful.

Soma Sara

Sara launched Everyone's Invited after posting about her experiences of sexual assault on her Instagram account. She called out examples of the sexism, misogyny, harassment and abuse that she had experienced at school, and in just one week she received more than 300 anonymous responses from those who'd had similar experiences.

In an interview with Harriet Hall (2021) in *The Independent,* Sara said that despite some resistance, the response from strangers and friends was overwhelming. They became the catalyst for setting up a safe space online for people to post anonymous submissions. Her campaign has now become international, with Australia and America beginning similar campaigns to reveal the sexual violence that seems to have become part of our culture, and has been exacerbated by social media.

I could have included any number of young, resourceful people on this list – Greta Thunberg; Liza Bilal and Naomi Smith, the incredible catalysts who orchestrated and mobilised the anti-racist movement in Bristol; or Nathan Law, the unlikely young figurehead of a pro-democracy movement in Hong Kong.

But I've chosen Sara to represent the impressive list of young people, with their mastery of social media, who are demonstrating how powerful they can be in terms of taking ownership. They use social media to create connectivity and build engaged communities, prompting their followers to action and highlighting the issues that matter to them the most. Sara has built a worldwide network and movement highlighting the insidious sexual abuse experienced by young people across the globe, creating a climate of fear and profoundly impacting relationships and lives.

That's why she's one of my scavenger heroes.

Trawden, Lancashire
(with special mention of Stephen Wilcock)

There has been plenty of press coverage about the regeneration of this extraordinary village by the people who live there. Once a thriving community with a local fabric mill providing employment, the village faced a gradual decline after the last of these mills closed back in the 1970s, later followed by the closure of a number of local businesses and churches.

Trawden's decline seemed to signal the end of its community spirit, as it risked turning into a ghost town. But one man was having none of it.

In 2014, Stephen Wilcock, Chair of the Trawden Community Trust, kick-started a campaign to buy the endangered community centre from the council, and did so for £1. It's now a bustling hub of activity offering classes in tai chi, a home to Brownie and Girl Guide groups and a venue for weddings and humanist funerals.

This success helped the community grow confidence in their ability to work together to achieve extraordinary things, and take ownership of their own wellbeing. In 2017, the trust purchased the library and won £350,000 for a renovation programme. They went on to turn a health centre into a thriving village shop designed to reduce plastic and unnecessary packaging. With the help of a population of just under 2,000, they raised enough money to buy the local pub and stop it from closing down. That too is now a lively hub for the community, and has been a huge success for the new tenants. More than 100 local volunteers help to run the village shop and library.

Trawden is an example of how much people are capable of when called to do something that matters, showing incredible resourcefulness, pragmatism and self-organisation. In one of the reports about Trawden's success, a local resident described the newly restored community spirit, volunteering opportunities and the new connections she had made as 'lifesaving' (Fenton 2022).

Trawden is living proof that we already have what we need. We just need to see that and release it, taking small steps to learn and grow.

Cliff Young

Every year, the elite runners of Australia line up to run a 543.7-mile race across rough terrain. This endurance test takes up to five days to finish, so only the fittest need apply. But back in 1983, a 61-year-old man stood at the starting line, dressed in working overalls and boots. No one who watched the start of that race thought he would last the day. Indeed, many thought it was some sort of prank.

But Cliff Young knew that he could do it. He may not have trained in the conventional way or had the expertise to support him. But he had lived on a 2,000-acre farm all his life, responsible even as a child for looking after 2,000 sheep, rounding them up and keeping them safe. He had resilience and stamina built in. Those who watched Young were amazed not only by his appearance, but by his shuffle. It couldn't really be called a run because his feet barely left the earth.

Suffice to say, while the hares sprang off from the starting line with gusto, tortoise Young shuffled along behind them at a steady, if slow pace. The runners knew they had to run for 18 hours, leaving just six hours to sleep. But Young didn't know that. He just kept going, through the day and night. Gradually, as the race wore on, Young caught up with the speedy runners, and in his slow, steady shuffle began to take over each and every one of them, emerging at the end of the race as the winner and setting a new world record.

Not knowing or being particularly interested in the rules of the race, he hadn't known that there would be a prize for the winner. When he was awarded £10,000, a bemused Young insisted on sharing the money with fellow runners.

Young went on to continue entering the race, eventually raising thousands for the homeless. He rightly became a legend and set a new course for the race: now runners keep running throughout the night, and many have adopted the 'Cliff Young Shuffle'. There are many reasons why Young is one of my scavenger heroes, but the most important one he has demonstrated is that if you don't know the rules, you can't be confined by them.

Push back boundaries and set your own course!

Volodymyr Zelenskyy

No one deserves to be called a hero more than this man. A few years ago, his leadership was seen as an oddity. He had been an actor who played a high-school teacher unexpectedly elected president of Ukraine – life imitating art to a ridiculous degree.

Zelenskyy comes from a highly educated family: his father a professor of computer science, his mother an engineer, and he has a law degree from Kyiv National Economic University. Perhaps it is this very breadth of experience that has helped to create this masterful leader, at once able to command considerable respect as a powerful communicator, engaging people on every level on the global stage.

But there are few people who demonstrate the power of scavenger leadership better than the president of Ukraine. When Russia invaded Ukraine, Zelenskyy turned down the US offer of evacuation from Kyiv, stating: 'The fight is here – I need ammunition, not a ride' (Braithwaite 2022).

At the time of writing, I have no idea what his fate or the fate of his country will be, neither indeed does the rest of Europe. Uncertainty has never reigned so supreme, and yet Zelenskyy, the actor/comedian-turned-president, has emerged as one of the most heroic leaders of recent times, inspiring his country and the rest of the world with his direct and honest stance.

His words are powerful, but his actions are even

more so. He has shown leadership that no degree can teach. This is instinctive, intuitive, resourceful and courageous leading in action. He has inspired people all over the world and brought his people with him, literally standing shoulder-to-shoulder with them in a way most leaders are incapable of doing.

All of us

The final entry in my list of scavenger heroes has to be *us* – all of us, and the possibilities we represent.

If we've learned nothing else over the past few years, it's that no one is ordinary. We're all capable of far more than we realise. Old-style leadership needs to evolve to keep up with the pace of today's wicked world. We can no longer afford to waste the potential that exists, financially or morally. There are enough resources, there is enough skill, we have enough to meet our needs. There is no need for leaders to feel burdened with impossible responsibility when they can benefit from greater, more informed collaboration.

The job of leader lies within us all, and we should be nurturing this in turn in our children. I believe they are the scavenger generation. My eldest daughter's year was the last to sit exams in a conventional way. Nothing is as it once was, and perhaps that's for the best. Let's help them to learn not to be afraid of the loss of certainty – to know that, in fact, it never really existed. Let's help them to trust in their own resourcefulness, and recognise that what really matters lies within.

To emerge from these dark times, we need new ideas, fresh energy and a greater sense of possibility to replace the rigidity of leaders who have failed to learn vital lessons. The scavenger mindset is within us all. It can unite us and bring out the very best in who we are and who we can be.

The scavenger mindset isn't for you; it *is* you.

Find your power so that you can shine a light on others, and together we can all achieve far more with very much less.

Final shout-out

I wanted to give a quick shout-out to some other scavenger leaders. In true scavenger fashion, I invite you to find out more about them and be inspired by what they've achieved and what they stand for. They've all given me something to think about, something to hope for, and have taught me something important:

Banksy, Niels Bohr, David Bowie, Tim Brown, Yvon Chouinard, Ben Cohen, Michaela Cohen, Jaz Coleman, Marie Curie, Brian Eno, Richard Feynman, Rosalind Franklin, Chris Gourlay, Jerry Greenfield, Gary Hamel, Daniel Levy, Ellen MacArthur, Jack Monroe, Caitlin Moran, Paul Oakenfold, Robert Owens, Marcus Rashford, Michael Rosen, E.F. Schumacher, Ricardo Semler, Lemn Sissay, Gareth Southgate, Fry Taylor, Booker T. Washington and Jacky Wright.

Acknowledgements

I'd like to take this opportunity to thank the myriad scavengers I've met, read about and been inspired by over the years. Scavengers rock. I've seen the scavenger in my children and my friends' children, in friends adapting to new challenges and, as the world has become more wicked, examples across the world of people using their ingenuity to manage difficult times, and finding such strength in those around them.

Special thanks must go to Helene Connolly. We've worked together on and off ever since the high-street project, and she has been immensely helpful with this book, as well as a vital supporter on the sidelines. I'd also like to thank Steve Boucher, who has been a constant source of support and encouragement, and a great friend since we studied together for the MA.

Massive thanks also to my editor, Beverley Glick. She has had to deal with my scavenger mindset and constant barrage of new thoughts and ideas, as well as my self-doubt. In Hardy-esque fashion, she's had to find a way to tame my wicked mind and find a narrative that will make sense to others.

Thanks to my siblings. It's been a tough year, and

they've generously stepped up when I haven't been available to offer the support needed in our family. Thanks to my dear, mighty mum, who has been stoic and brave in the face of her terrible illness, one that's so cruelly familiar to her, arriving after she'd faced one of the most horrendous years imaginable. Her hallmark grace, intelligence and pragmatism are as clear today as they were when I was small.

Finally, thanks to my extraordinary daughters. They have both shown support in their own unique ways, with real wisdom and insight. My girls demonstrate to me every day that they're instinctive scavengers. They're finding their own way in life and doing so with such maturity, despite the uncertainties of a fast-changing world. They focus on what they can do, make the most of what they have, and enjoy today without letting their dreams and ambitions disappear. They've had their fair share of tough situations to deal with, and have learned some coping mechanisms that I hope will hold them in good stead. They remind me that when we say children are resilient, we only really find that out when they're adults. They understand that when you have a strong core, change isn't something to be frightened of but embraced. They represent the generation that we need to take us forward into a better world. Both girls were top of mind as I wrote this book, and one day I hope they might read it!

Resources

Addams, J. (1910) *Twenty Years at Hull House.* Macmillan.

Alinsky, S. (1971) *Rules for Radicals.* Vintage.

Ariely, D. (2011) *The Upside of Irrationality: The unexpected benefits of defying logic and work and home.* HarperCollins.

Badonsky, J. (2013) *The Muse Is In.* Running Press.

Braithwaite, S. (2022) 'Zelensky refuses US offer to evacuate, saying "I need ammunition, not a ride"'. *CNN*, 26 February. Available at: https://edition.cnn.com/2022/02/26/europe/ukraine-zelensky-evacuation-intl/index.html, accessed 18.5.22.

Brown, M. (2015) *The Man Who Knew Infinity.* Warner Bros.

Burton, T.I. (2015) 'Could you be a Super Forecaster?'. BBC, 20 January. Available at: www.bbc.com/future/article/20150120-are-you-a-super-forecaster, accessed 18.5.2022.

Campbell, D. (2018) 'Liverpool NHS Trust "dysfunctional" and unsafe, report finds'. *The Guardian*, 8 February. Available at: www.theguardian.com/society/2018/feb/08/

liverpool-nhs-trust-dysfunctional-and-unsafe-report-finds, accessed 18.5.22.

Carreyrou, J. (2018) *Bad Blood: Secrets and lies in a Silicon Valley startup.* Picador.

Chamine, S. (2016) *Positive Intelligence.* Greenleaf Book Group Press.

Chapman, B. & Sisodia, R. (2015) *Everybody Matters: The extraordinary power of caring for your people like family.* Penguin Random House.

Doyle, A. Conan (2011[1927]) *The Case-Book of Sherlock Holmes.* Penguin.

Drexler, K.E. & Minsky, M. (1987) *Engines of Creation: The coming era of nanotechnology.* Anchor Books.

Easterbrook, G. (2004) *The Progress Paradox.* Random House Trade Publications.

Edmondson, A. (1999) 'Psychological safety and learning behaviour in work teams'. *Administrative Science Quarterly* 44(2) 350–383.

Elliot, J. & Sullivan, L. (2015) 'How the Red Cross raised half billion dollars for Haiti and built six homes', ProPublica, 3 June. Available at: www.propublica.org/article/how-the-red-cross-raised-half-a-billion-dollars-for-haiti-and-built-6-homes, accessed 18.5.22.

Fenton, R. (2022) 'Village where residents banded together to buy the pub, library and post office'. *Daily Mirror*, 10 January. Available at: www.mirror.

co.uk/news/weird-news/village-residents-worked-together-buy-25904709, accessed 18.5.22.

Fredrickson, B.L. (2003) 'The value of positive emotions'. *American Scientist*. Available at: www.americanscientist.org/sites/americanscientist.org/files/20058214332_306.pdf, accessed 18.5.22.

Gates, T. (2015) 'How to revive a neighborhood: with imagination, beauty, and art'. *TED Talks* 26 March. Available at: www.youtube.com/watch?v=S9ry1M7JlyE, accessed 18.5.22.

Gilbert, E. (2015) *Big Magic*. Bloomsbury.

Grint, K. & Holt, C. (2011) 'Leading questions: If "total place", '"Big Society" and local leadership are the answers, what's the question?' *Leadership* 7(1) 85–98.

Grint, K. & Holt, C. (2012) 'Leadership, followership, and problems'. *Network Review Writer* (Winter) 20–23.

Haidt, J. (2006) *The Happiness Hypothesis: Finding modern truth in ancient wisdom*. Basic Books.

Hall, H. (2021) 'Soma Sara has an inbox full of allegations about sexual violence in the UK: It's time to listen'. *The Independent*, 1 April. Available at: independent.co.uk/lifestyle/women, accessed 9.5.22.

Hamel, G. (2009) '25 stretch goals for management'. *Harvard Business Review*, 3 February. Available at:

https://hbr.org/2009/02/25-stretch-goals-for-managemen, accessed 18.5.22.

Hazy, J.K., Goldstein, J.A. & Lichtenstein, B.B. (2007) *Complex Systems Leadership Theory: New perspectives from complexity science on social and organizational effectiveness* 1. ISCE Publishing.

Heath, C. & Heath, D. (2010) *Switch: How to change things when change is hard.* Random House.

Heuer, R., Jr (1999) *Psychology of Intelligence Analysis.* Center for the Study of Intelligence, Central Intelligence Agency.

Holbeche, L. (2015) *The Agile Organization.* Kogan Page.

Kirkup, B. (2018) 'Report of the Liverpool Community Health Independent Review', 8 February. Available at: www.england.nhs.uk/publication/report-of-the-liverpool-community-health-independent-review/, accessed 18.5.22.

Kline, N. (1999) *Time to Think.* Ward Lock.

Laloux, F. (2014) *Reinventing Organisations: A guide to creating organizations inspired by the next stage of human consciousness.* Nelson Parker.

Maslow, A.H. (1943) 'A theory of human motivation'. *Psychological Review* 50 370–396.

Massachusetts General Hospital & Harvard Medical School (2015) 'Study of adult development'. Available at: https://www.adultdevelopment-study.org/grantandglueckstudy, accessed 18.5.22.

McGregor, D. (2008) 'Theory X and Y: Toward a construct valid measure'. *Journal of Managerial Issues* 20(2) 255–271.

McKnight, J. & Block, P. (2010) *The Abundant Community: Awakening the power of families and neighborhoods.* Berrett-Koehler Publishers Inc.

Mead, R. (2020) 'George the Poet's undefinably good podcast'. *The New Yorker,* 8 March. Available at: https://www.newyorker.com/culture/podcast-dept/george-the-poets-undefinably-good-podcast, accessed 9.5.22.

Mitchell Waldrop, M. (1996) 'The trillion dollar vision of Dee Hock'. *Fast Company,* 31 October. Available at: www.fastcompany.com/27333/trillion-dollar-vision-dee-hock, accessed 22.4.22.

Petzinger, T., Jr (1999) *The New Pioneers: The men and women who are transforming the workplace and marketplace.* Simon & Schuster.

Post, G.S. (2005) 'Altruism, happiness and health; It's good to be good'. *International Journal of Behavioural Medicine* 12(2) 66–77. Available at: https://greatergood.berkeley.edu/images/uploads/Post-AltruismHappinessHealth.pdf, accessed 18.5.22.

Pransky, J. (2003) *Prevention from the Inside-out.* 1st Books Library.

Pranksy, J. (2011) *Modello: A story of hope for the inner-city and beyond: An inside-out model of prevention and resiliency in action.* CCB Publishing.

Radjou, N. & Prabhu, J. (2016) *Frugal Innovation: How to do more with less*. Profile Books.

Rittel, H.W.J. & Webber, M.M. (1973) 'Dilemmas in general theory of planning'. *Policy Science* 4 155–156.

Robinson, J. (2021) 'From faded seaside spot turned hipsters' paradise to a northern resort now a "des res"…'. *MailOnline*, 27 December. Available at: www.dailymail.co.uk/news/article-10292637/Portas-Review-towns-doing-decade-project-aiming-save-Britains-high-streets.html, accessed 18.5.22.

Sarasrathy, S. (2008) *Elements of Entrepreneurial Expertise*. Edward Elgar Publishing.

Seligman, M. (2002) *Authentic Happiness*. John Murray Press.

Semler, R. (1993) *Maverick!* Random House.

Senge, P. (2006) *The Fifth Discipline: The art and practice of the learning organization*. Random House.

Shale, S. (2018) 'The Independent review of workplace culture at Save the Children UK: Final report'. Available at: www.savethechildren.org.uk/content/dam/gb/reports/independent-review-of-workplace-culture-at-save-the-children-uk.pdf, accessed 18.5.22.

Sohn, E. (2021) 'How one woman convinced a community to love a bad omen'. *Yes!*, 15 March. Available at: www.yesmagazine.org/

environment/2021/03/15/india-species-conservation, accessed 9.5.22.

Thorpe, V. (2021) 'George the Poet: "It's easier to change the lives of offenders in prison than it is on the outside"'. *The Observer*, 7 November. Available at: www.theguardian.com/culture/2021/nov/07/george-the-poet-its-easier-to-change-the-lives-of-offenders-in-prison-than-it-is-outside, accessed 18.5.22.

Trott, D. (2019) *Creative Blindness (and How to Cure It): Real life stories of remarkable creative vision.* Harriman House.

Veisdal, J. (2021) 'Ramanujan's first letter to G.H. Hardy (1913)'. *Privatdozent*, 1 June. Available at: https://www.privatdozent.co/p/ramanujans-first-letter-to-gh-hardy-1d9?s=r, accessed 18.5.22.

Vuori, TO and Hu, QN (2015) 'Distributed attention and shared emotions in the innovation process: How Nokia lost the smartphone battle'. *Administrative Science Quarterly* 61(1): 9–51.

Warhurst, P. & Dobson, J. (2014) *Incredible! Plant veg, grow a revolution.* Matador.

Web of Stories (2017) 'Sydney Brenner – Scientific interaction with Francis Crick (66/236)'. *YouTube*, 5 July. Available at: www.youtube.com/watch?v=kiihcWOcs5A, accessed 18.5.22.

Wheatley, M.J. ((2006) *Leadership and the New Science.* Berrett-Koehler Publishers Inc.

Zeitlin, M. (2019) 'Why WeWork went wrong'. *The Guardian*, 20 December. Available at: www.theguardian.com/business/2019/dec/20/why-wework-went-wrong, accessed 18.5.22.